EXPRESS DINNERS

175 DELICIOUS MEALS YOU CAN MAKE IN 30 MINUTES OR LESS

EXPRESS DINNERS

175 DELICIOUS MEALS YOU CAN MAKE IN 30 MINUTES OR LESS

LIZ FRANKLIN

DUNCAN BAIRD PUBLISHERS

LONDON

Express Dinners
Liz Franklin

Distributed in the USA and Canada by
Sterling Publishing Co., Inc.
387 Park Avenue South
New York, NY 10016-8810

First published in the UK and USA in 2012 by
Duncan Baird Publishers Ltd
Sixth Floor, Castle House
75–76 Wells Street, London W1T 3QH

Managing Editor: Grace Cheetham
Editor: Nicola Graimes
Americanizer: Norma MacMillan
Managing Designer: Manisha Patel
Designer: Gail Jones
Commissioned Photography: Toby Scott
Food Stylist: Kate Blinman
Prop Stylist: Clare Hunt

Library of Congress Cataloging-in-Publication Data available

ISBN: 978-1-84899-026-5

10 9 8 7 6 5 4 3 2 1

Typeset in Rockwell
Color reproduction by XY Digital
Printed in Singapore by Imago

For information about custom editions, special sales, premium and
corporate purchases, please contact Sterling Special Sales
Department at 800-805-5489 or specialsales@sterlingpub.com.

Publisher's note
While every care has been taken in compiling the recipes for this
book, Duncan Baird Publishers, or any other persons who have been
involved in working on this publication, cannot accept responsibility
for any errors or omissions, inadvertent or not, that may be found in the
recipes or text, nor for any problems that may arise as a result of
preparing one of these recipes or following the advice contained in
this work. If you are pregnant or breastfeeding or have any special
dietary requirements or medical conditions, it is important to consult a
medical professional before following any of the recipes in this book.
Ill or elderly people, babies, young children and women who are
pregnant or breastfeeding should avoid any recipes containing lightly
cooked eggs.

Acknowledgments
With huge thanks to Grace Cheetham, Nicola Graimes and the team at
DBP for helping to turn *Express Dinners* into such a beautiful book—
and to Toby Scott, Kate Blinman and Clare Hunt for the beautiful
photography. Also, masses of love and thanks to my wonderful parents
and my three sons, Chris, Oli and Tim, for their love, support and
encouragement in everything I do.

Notes on the recipes
Unless otherwise stated:
All recipes serve 4
Use large eggs
Use medium fruit and vegetables
Use fresh ingredients, including herbs and chilies
1 tsp. = 5ml 1 tbsp. = 15ml 1 cup = 240ml

CONTENTS

6   INTRODUCTION

10   FIVE-MINUTE MEALS

34   TEN-MINUTE MEALS

58   FIFTEEN-MINUTE MEALS

84   TWENTY-MINUTE MEALS

108   TWENTY-FIVE-MINUTE MEALS

132   THIRTY-MINUTE MEALS

158   INDEX

INTRODUCTION

For most of us, time is something we never seem to have enough of. We're so wrapped up in the hustle and bustle of our busy lives that cooking often becomes an afterthought—it's tempting just to grab a take-out, or buy something to pop in the microwave. But producing a quick, nutritious meal needn't take an age or be complicated, and it can certainly be enjoyable. Fast food can be fun food!

The collection of recipes in *Express Dinners* shows how you can create a meal from scratch using fresh ingredients in anything from five to thirty minutes. It really is possible to cook up something sensational in the time it would take to pick up a take-out or heat a prepared meal; and it's not only doable but also rewarding.

There is so much to gain from getting into the kitchen and rustling up anything from a simple dinner to a fantastic feast for friends. Sitting down together—eating, chatting, listening, laughing and catching up with friends and family—is precious. The stresses and strains of a hurried day can seem halved, or the excitement of good news

doubled, when we sit down to share a great meal in good company.

ABOUT THE RECIPES

One of the most important features of *Express Dinners* is that all the recipes are "complete" meals, so they contain all the components necessary for a well-balanced dinner. Reassuringly, this means that each recipe features any accompaniments, whether it is pasta, rice, potatoes, beans or simply crusty bread, as well as side dishes such as vegetables or salad; and crucially each one can be made from start to table within the time contraints—whether it is five minutes or thirty minutes.

Inspired by the cuisines of the world, there should be a recipe in this book to whet your appetite, no matter what you're in the mood to eat! A wide variety of ingredients is now more readily available than ever before, so it's possible to create my recipes for a fragrant Golden Ginger Duck, Mexican Bean Chile with Avocado Cream, or Moroccan Fish Tagine, for example, with ease and in next to no time. What's more, taking charge of what you eat enables you to ensure meals are fresh and nutritious, and not loaded with any unwanted additives.

The more we realize just how much enjoyment, satisfaction and fantastic food can come out of spending even a short amount of time in the kitchen, the more enthusiastic and confident we are likely to become about cooking. So I've put together lots of fabulous, fuss-free recipes that are made from simple, easily obtainable ingredients, whether you're looking to make a speedy after-work meal or something a little more special.

There are no long-simmered stocks, complicated sauces or mind-bogglingly long lists of ingredients either. When time is at a premium, no one wants to spend hours in the supermarket searching for hard-to-find ingredients. There are substantial salads, mouthwatering meat dishes, delectable fish-feasts and meals for vegetarians that meat-eaters will find hard to resist, too. And I've also added tips that will help to make your time in the kitchen as enjoyable and stress-free as possible.

PANTRY BASICS

For the cook in a hurry, a well-stocked pantry becomes a real treasure trove.

Fill it with ingredients that you use on a regular basis in order to make life easier and meals more varied. Now's the time to clear out those half-empty packages of something bought many years ago; spices that are so past their best that their flavor is long gone; or jars of powders and pastes purchased for one-off recipes that now look decidedly unpalatable.

Ideally, treat the pantry as a significant part of your kitchen—make it a stash of indispensable basics that you can build upon. So if it looks like something from *The Land That Time Forgot*, give it a good clear out and start over!

Stock your pantry with handy basics that will enable you to produce the kinds of meals you love to eat, time and time again. Staples such as canned tomatoes, canned beans, pasta and Asian noodles, rice, lentils, quick-cook grains, jars of tomato purée, punchy pastes for curries, a small selection of everyday spices, and of course those essential seasonings, salt and pepper, are all a must.

Always have extra-virgin olive oil on hand—ideally a blended one for cooking, plus something a little more special for drizzling over meat, fish or vegetables, as well as dressing salads, and even to serve as a dip with vegetables and bread as an easy, pre-dinner appetizer.

A bottle each of balsamic, red and white wine vinegar will always come in handy, and jars of roasted red bell peppers, artichoke hearts, olives, capers and anchovies are brilliant for adding a little oomph to all manner of dishes. For Asian-style suppers, key ingredients such as toasted sesame oil and soy, fish and sweet chili sauces are also indispensable.

So, with a little organization and planning, you will have the basics to whip up quick and tasty meals.

SHREWD SHOPPING

A hectic lifestyle means that most of us need to shop in the most time-effective and expedient way. For many of us that means large stores and supermarkets, but it's not always possible to fit in a quick visit in the middle of a busy day. And how many of us want to face a rushed and frenetic shop at the end of a long day at work?

Shopping online may save time and is certainly useful for bulk or long-lasting items, but it is easy to switch onto autopilot and become very repetitive in our shopping habits. Choosing fresh fruit, vegetables, meat or fish is better done in person, and sometimes it may be quicker to pop into a local butcher or food market, if you are lucky enough to have them nearby. It's also good

to support the smaller local stores and farmer's markets. Even the busiest of us might make time to sow a few seeds in a pot to give a supply of fresh herbs on the kitchen windowsill—it doesn't take as long as you think and it's economical and fun!

In a move to eat well in less time, it's a good idea to try to stay in tune with the seasons when buying fresh fruit and vegetables. That way, you can also keep costs down and ensure that meals are as nutritious and tasty as possible. What's more, when buying loose fresh produce you negate the need for unnecessary packaging.

It's also worth considering that packaged prepared meals often contain unwanted additives, many of which have been linked to health problems. By buying good-quality ingredients and preparing fresh food yourself, you have much more control over all these vital considerations—and mealtimes become special again, rather than being a rushed affair simply for the purpose of re-fueling.

For the time-pressured cook, it makes absolute sense to get the best from your supplier, wherever you choose to shop. When you're buying fish, for example, whether from a specialist fish man or at the supermarket, make sure it has been cleaned and prepared as well as filleted and skinned or scaled, if required. Ask the butcher to trim meat to remove unnecessary fat and bones and do other preparation needed. Any supplier worth their salt will be pleased to offer a good service.

BE ADAPTABLE

Don't be afraid to substitute ingredients when following the recipes in this book. If you can't get exactly what is specified in the recipe, or you want to use one of your favorite ingredients instead of what is listed, you can consider the characteristics of the dish and the cooking method, rather than following it in every detail. That way, you can adjust and adapt to suit your preferences.

If the recipe suggests an accompaniment, don't feel you need to be precise, especially with simple things such as bread, salad greens or vegetables. They are only suggestions and it's best to follow your own personal preferences and what you have on hand. Think about ingredients that make good partners in terms of texture and flavor—although you must remember to factor in the cooking times, too. There's no point planning to serve roast potatoes alongside something from the 10-minute chapter. The more you cook, the more expert your palate and kitchen skills will become, and the more your intuition will guide you.

BE PREPARED

For those of you who are fairly new to cooking, some of the recipes may take a little longer at the start, but relax, enjoy and have confidence in your ability to make great, tasty meals—and you're sure to become speedier soon!

For all levels of ability, it goes without saying that the buzzword for the busy cook is undoubtedly ''be prepared'' (okay, well two words). A major cause of delay (and frustration) when cooking is finding that you're midway through preparing a dish, and you don't have everything you need. Scrabbling around in the cupboards or rummaging through the fridge to look for a vital ingredient, only to find subsequently that you don't have it, is something we probably all do at some stage, but it really doesn't help create calm and harmony in the kitchen.

Plan meals ahead, decide what you are going to cook, read through the whole recipe before you start, and get all the ingredients and tools you need to hand. To be organized is to be halfway there.

So, all that remains to be said is that I hope you enjoy cooking and eating your way through the recipes that follow as much as I did developing and writing them—and that you will very soon discover that less time doesn't mean less tempting or less tasty!

FIVE MINUTES DOESN'T SOUND MUCH TIME TO PREPARE AND COOK A MEAL, BUT IT REALLY CAN BE DONE! USING TEMPTING TIME SAVERS, SUCH AS SMOKED FISH, SPECIFIC CUTS OF MEAT, AND FRESH PASTA, IT'S POSSIBLE TO CREATE A RANGE OF MOUTHWATERING MEALS, INCLUDING MINUTE STEAKS WITH BLUE CHEESE SAUCE AND SMOKED SALMON TAGLIATELLE.

FIVE-
MINUTE
MEALS

SMOKED CHICKEN, AVOCADO & WALNUT SALAD

Smoked chicken adds a deliciously different touch to this salad, but you could use cold roast chicken as an alternative.

4 ready-to-eat skinless, boneless smoked chicken breasts, shredded • 4 large handfuls of arugula leaves • 2 ripe avocados, pitted and sliced • 2 handfuls of walnut halves
DRESSING: 6 tablespoons extra-virgin olive oil • 2 tablespoons red wine vinegar • 1 teaspoon wholegrain mustard • a pinch of sugar • salt and freshly ground black pepper

TO SERVE: crusty bread

1 Put the chicken in a large salad bowl. Add the arugula leaves and avocado, then scatter the walnuts over the top.
2 Put all the ingredients for the dressing into a tightly capped jar, season with a little salt and pepper, and shake well until the dressing emulsifies. Pour enough of the dressing over the salad to coat lightly, then toss well. Serve with slices of crusty bread.

CHICKEN NOODLE SOUP

Thai tom yum paste, which can be found in Asian markets and from online sources, makes a useful and versatile flavoring for soups and other Thai dishes. Adjust the amount to suit your personal preference, starting with just a teaspoonful of paste and then adding more to taste, so that you don't end up over-doing it.

6 cups chicken stock • 1 to 2 teaspoons tom yum paste, or to taste • 7 ounces cooked, skinless, boneless chicken breast, cut into strips (about 1½ cups) • 2 packages dried ramen noodles (without the seasoning) or 11 ounces fresh Asian noodles • 2 handfuls of sugar snap peas • 6 scallions, chopped

1 Pour the chicken stock into a large saucepan and stir in the tom yum paste. Bring to a boil, then turn the heat down and add the chicken and noodles. Simmer the soup 2 to 3 minutes, stirring from time to time to separate the noodles.
2 Add the sugar snap peas to the pan with the scallions, then cook 1 minute longer before serving in bowls.

SPINACH, PROSCIUTTO & EGG SALAD

The saltiness of crisp prosciutto marries beautifully with tender spinach leaves. Add a runny fried egg on top and this becomes an amazingly quick but comforting meal.

3 tablespoons olive oil • 4 extra-large eggs • 8 slices prosciutto • 4 large handfuls of baby spinach leaves • 10½ ounces jarred mixed wild mushrooms in olive oil, drained • 8 sun-dried tomatoes in olive oil, drained and coarsely chopped • 1 to 2 teaspoons balsamic vinegar • salt and freshly ground black pepper

TO SERVE: baguette

1 Heat the olive oil in a large, nonstick frying pan over medium heat. Fry the eggs until the white is set but the yolk remains runny, 3 to 4 minutes.
2 Meanwhile, heat a separate nonstick frying pan over high heat. Fry the prosciutto, turning once, until crisp and golden, 1 to 2 minutes.
3 At the same time, put the spinach in a large salad bowl. Add the mushrooms, sun-dried tomatoes and balsamic vinegar. Season with salt and pepper, then toss well until combined.
4 Serve the salad on individual plates, topped with a fried egg and prosciutto, with slices of baguette on the side.

PROSCIUTTO, PECORINO & GREEN LEAF SALAD

Salty prosciutto and crumbly pecorino combine perfectly with sweet, tangy balsamic vinegar and peppery salad greens.

4 large handfuls of mixed salad greens (including spinach, arugula and watercress, if possible) • 12 slices of prosciutto, torn into pieces • 5 ounces aged pecorino cheese
DRESSING: 6 tablespoons extra-virgin olive oil • 2 tablespoons balsamic vinegar • salt and freshly ground black pepper

TO SERVE: breadsticks

1 Put the salad greens in a serving bowl and top with the prosciutto. Using a vegetable peeler, slice the pecorino into shavings and add to the bowl.
2 To make the dressing, whisk the olive oil and balsamic vinegar together and season with salt and pepper.
3 Add enough of the dressing to coat the leaves lightly and toss everything well. Serve the salad with breadsticks on the side.

HOT MORTADELLA PANINI

These panini are best served warm so the fat from the mortadella melts into the bread, making it moist and tasty. Fans of spicy food will love a drizzle of chili oil, too.

4 ciabatta rolls, cut in half • 8 slices of mortadella sausage • ¾ cup roasted red bell peppers in olive oil, drained and sliced • 1 small bunch of watercress • lemon juice or chili oil, for drizzling (optional)

TO SERVE: Italian-style green salad

1 Preheat the broiler.
2 Toast the ciabatta, crust-side up, under the broiler until light golden, 1 to 2 minutes. Turn over and toast the other side lightly, about 1 minute.
3 Top one half of each ciabatta roll with the mortadella, roasted peppers and watercress, then squeeze a little lemon juice over or drizzle on chili oil, if using. Place the other half of the ciabatta roll on top and serve with an Italian-style salad of mixed greens.

BROILED SALAMI PITA PIZZAS

These pizzas make a great speedy and satisfying impromptu meal.

6 tablespoons good-quality tomato purée or tomato sauce • ½ teaspoon dried oregano • 4 round pita breads • 7 ounces mozzarella cheese, drained and torn into pieces • 12 slices of salami • 1 tablespoon extra-virgin olive oil • a few baby salad greens • salt and freshly ground black pepper

TO SERVE: mixed leaf salad

1 Preheat the broiler.
2 Mix the tomato purée with the oregano. Spoon this sauce on top of the pita breads and spread out evenly, leaving a border clear. Scatter the mozzarella over the sauce, season with salt and pepper, and top with the salami.
3 Drizzle a little olive oil over each pizza and broil, close to the heat, until the cheese is bubbling and melted, about 2 minutes. Scatter a few baby salad greens over the top and serve with a mixed leaf salad.

BRESAOLA & ARTICHOKE SALAD

Bresaola is an Italian specialty made from lean beef cured in a very particular way, producing a gorgeous meat that is very low in fat. Speck or prosciutto would also work well as alternatives.

16 slices of bresaola • 12 ounces jarred artichoke hearts in olive oil, drained • 4 ounces Parmesan cheese • 1 lemon, cut into thin wedges • 2 tablespoons extra-virgin olive oil • 1 tablespoon chopped parsley leaves (optional) • freshly ground black pepper

TO SERVE: sun-dried tomato and olive focaccia bread

1 Arrange the bresaola on a serving platter and top with the artichoke hearts. Using a vegetable peeler, slice the Parmesan into shavings and scatter over the top.
2 Squeeze the juice from 1 to 2 lemon wedges over the salad, or to taste. Arrange the remaining lemon wedges around the platter. Drizzle on the olive oil and season with pepper. Sprinkle with parsley, if using, before serving with slices of focaccia.

MINUTE STEAKS WITH BLUE CHEESE SAUCE >

This rich and creamy blue cheese sauce takes next to no time to make and is delicious with tender steak. You could also try other types of blue cheese, if preferred.

5 ounces Gorgonzola cheese, crumbled • 4 tablespoons dry white wine • 3 to 4 small thyme sprigs • 4 minute steaks • 1 tablespoon olive oil • salt and freshly ground black pepper

TO SERVE: watercress salad and walnut bread

1 To make the sauce, put the Gorgonzola, wine and thyme sprigs in a small saucepan. Cook over medium heat, stirring occasionally, until the Gorgonzola has melted and the sauce is smooth and creamy, 2 to 3 minutes. Season with salt and pepper.
2 Meanwhile, heat a ridged grill pan until very hot. Brush the steaks with the olive oil, season with salt and pepper and grill 1 minute on each side.
3 Spoon the sauce over the steaks and serve immediately with a watercress salad and slices of walnut bread.

TUNA & BEAN SALAD

This works well with canned tuna in oil, but for the best flavor look for top-quality tuna that is packed in extra-virgin olive oil.

4 large handfuls of mixed salad greens • 14 ounces jarred or canned tuna fillets in extra-virgin olive oil, drained and flaked into chunks • 14 ounces canned cannellini beans, drained and rinsed • 1 ripe beefsteak tomato, seeded and roughly chopped • 1 small onion, chopped • 1 small handful of chopped parsley leaves • 4 tablespoons extra-virgin olive oil • juice of ½ lemon, or to taste • salt and freshly ground black pepper

TO SERVE: olive ciabatta bread

1 Put the salad greens in a serving bowl. Add the tuna, cannellini beans, tomato, onion and parsley.
2 Mix together the olive oil and lemon juice, then spoon it over the salad. Season with salt and pepper, then gently toss everything together. Serve with slices of olive ciabatta.

< TUNA CARPACCIO WITH CAPER DRESSING

The colder the tuna, the easier it is to cut into paper-thin slices. Or you could ask your fish merchant to slice the tuna for you.

6 tablespoons extra-virgin olive oil • 1 handful of salted capers, rinsed and drained • 11 ounces very cold, sushi-grade whole tuna loin, cut into very thin slices • juice of ½ lemon • 4 handfuls of arugula leaves

TO SERVE: lemon wedges and wholegrain bread

1 Heat 2 tablespoons of the olive oil in a small, nonstick frying pan until very hot. Add the capers and fry until puffed up, about 30 seconds. Remove the capers from the pan and drain on a paper towel.
2 Arrange the sliced tuna on four serving plates.
3 Put the capers into a bowl and stir in the remaining olive oil and the lemon juice until combined. Spoon this dressing over the tuna.
4 Top each serving with a handful of arugula leaves and a lemon wedge. Serve with slices of bread.

SMOKED SALMON TAGLIATELLE

This makes an elegant dinner, and its brief preparation and cooking will leave lots of time for you to spend with your guests.

1 pound 2 ounces fresh egg tagliatelle • ½ cup heavy cream • finely grated zest of 1 lemon • 1 tablespoon snipped chives • 9 ounces smoked salmon pieces • salt and freshly ground black pepper

TO SERVE: baby spinach leaf salad

1 Bring a large saucepan of salted water to a boil and cook the tagliatelle until al dente, about 2 minutes.
2 Meanwhile, gently heat the heavy cream with the lemon zest and chives in a large saucepan until warmed through, about 1 minute. Season with salt and pepper.
3 Using pasta tongs, lift the cooked pasta from the pan and add to the warm cream mixture. Add the salmon and turn until combined. Serve immediately with a baby spinach leaf salad.

SMOKED TROUT, SUGAR SNAP & AVOCADO SALAD

Packed with flavor and bursting with vitamins and beneficial fats, this salad makes a super-healthy and very quickly prepared dinner.

8 smoked trout fillets, skinned and flaked into large chunks • 2 handfuls of sugar snap peas • 2 ripe avocados, pitted and thinly sliced • juice of 1 lime • 4 tablespoons avocado oil • freshly ground black pepper

TO SERVE: seeded bread

1 Put the trout, sugar snap peas and avocado in a serving bowl.
2 Add the lime juice and drizzle the avocado oil over. Season with pepper and gently turn until combined. Serve the salad with slices of seeded bread.

SEARED SCALLOP & PEA SHOOT SALAD

Choose fresh diver scallops from a reliable fish merchant for this vibrant salad—frozen scallops may be plumped up with water and tend to shrink when cooked.

4 tablespoons extra-virgin olive oil • 12 fresh sea scallops • ½ teaspoon ginger paste • ½ teaspoon sugar • a pinch of dried chili flakes • juice of 1 lime • 4 handfuls of pea shoots • 1 handful of snow peas • coarse sea salt

TO SERVE: lime wedges and baguette

1 Heat 1 tablespoon of the olive oil in a ridged grill pan over high heat. Season the scallops with a little salt, then sear them for 1 minute on each side.
2 Mix together the ginger paste, sugar, chili flakes, lime juice and the remaining olive oil.
3 Place the pea shoots and snow peas in a large bowl, then pour the dressing over and toss well. Serve the scallops immediately with the salad, lime wedges and slices of baguette.

SALT & CHILI SQUID WITH LIME

Tasty and simple, this recipe makes a great light meal served with a mixed greens and herb salad. Alternatively, a salad of crunchy, Asian-style vegetables would also be delicious.

12 cleaned and prepared squid (calamari), cut into 2-inch pieces, and tentacles reserved • 2 to 3 tablespoons olive oil • ½ teaspoon dried chili flakes, or to taste • 2 scallions, minced • juice of 1 lime • 1 tablespoon chopped cilantro • salt and freshly ground black pepper

TO SERVE: lime wedges, green salad with herbs, and crusty bread

1 Score a diamond pattern lightly across the pieces of squid using the tip of a sharp knife.
2 Heat the olive oil in a wok or large, nonstick frying pan over high heat. Stir-fry the squid pieces and tentacles 1 minute. Add the chili flakes and scallions, then cook until the squid is just opaque, about 1 minute.
3 Add the lime juice and season with salt and pepper. Scatter the cilantro over and serve with lime wedges, a salad of mixed greens and herbs, and slices of crusty bread.

CHEAT'S GARLIC SHRIMP & BEANS

This makes a tasty and filling main course.

1 ripe beefsteak tomato, seeded and roughly chopped • 4 tablespoons extra-virgin olive oil • 2 garlic cloves, minced • 1 pound cooked, peeled extra-large or large shrimp • 14 ounces canned cannellini beans, drained and rinsed • 1 handful of chopped parsley leaves • salt and freshly ground black pepper

TO SERVE: arugula salad and crusty bread

1 Put the tomato, olive oil and garlic in a nonstick saucepan and heat gently, stirring occasionally, until warmed through, about 1 minute.
2 Put the shrimp in a serving bowl and add the cannellini beans.
3 Pour the warm dressing over the shrimp and beans, season with salt and pepper, and stir in the parsley. Serve with an arugula salad and slices of crusty bread.

CRAB & ANGEL HAIR PASTA >

Quick, delicate and very special, crab and angel hair pasta make a fine meal—even in just 5 minutes!

1 pound fresh angel hair pasta (capelli d'angelo) • 2 tablespoons extra-virgin olive oil • finely grated zest of 1 lemon • 1 pound cooked crab meat • 1 tablespoon chopped parsley leaves • salt and freshly ground black pepper

TO SERVE: lemon wedges and a green salad

1 Bring a large saucepan of salted water to a boil and cook the angel hair pasta until al dente, about 2 minutes, then drain and tip into a serving bowl.
2 While the pasta is cooking, mix together the olive oil and lemon zest.
3 Pour the lemon oil over the pasta and add the crab and parsley. Gently turn the pasta until combined, then season with salt and pepper. Serve with lemon wedges and a salad of mixed greens.

< SHRIMP & THREE-PEA STIR-FRY

Super-convenient ginger paste can be bought in jars from some supermarkets and Asian markets as well as from online suppliers.

11 ounces thin rice stick noodles • 2 tablespoons sunflower oil • 4 scallions, roughly chopped • 4 handfuls of sugar snap peas • 2 large handfuls of pea shoots • 1⅓ cups frozen peas • 14 ounces cooked, peeled but tail on jumbo or extra-large shrimp • 2 teaspoons ginger paste • 2 teaspoons honey • juice of 1 lime • 1 handful of cilantro leaves

TO SERVE: lime wedges

1 Place the noodles in a heatproof bowl and cover with boiling water. Stir, cover and set aside until soft, about 3 minutes.
2 Meanwhile, heat the sunflower oil in a wok over high heat. Stir-fry the scallions, sugar snap peas, pea shoots and peas 2 minutes.
3 Add the shrimp, then stir in the ginger paste, honey and lime juice. Cook until heated though, about 1 minute.
4 Drain the noodles, then add to the wok with the cilantro and toss until combined. Serve with lime wedges on the side.

SPICED TOMATO SHRIMP

Canned cherry tomatoes are an invaluable addition to the pantry and one of my favorites for rustling up all manner of tasty meals—my cupboard feels a lack without them!

1 tablespoon olive oil • 1 garlic clove, minced • 1 teaspoon fennel seeds • 14 ounces canned cherry tomatoes, drained • ½ teaspoon sugar • 1 pound cooked, peeled extra-large or large shrimp • 7 ounces feta cheese, crumbled • salt and freshly ground black pepper

TO SERVE: green salad and pita breads

1 Heat the olive oil in a large, nonstick frying pan over medium heat. Fry the garlic and fennel seeds 30 seconds.
2 Add the cherry tomatoes and sugar, season with salt and pepper, and cook, stirring occasionally, until the tomatoes begin to soften and break down, about 2 minutes.
3 Stir in the shrimp and feta, then cook just until heated through, about 1 minute. Serve with a salad of mixed greens and pita breads.

MOZZARELLA, TOMATO & ARUGULA SALAD

The secret to making this salad a success lies in the quality of the mozzarella and the olive oil—use buffalo mozzarella and a good fruity extra-virgin olive oil and the results will be deliciously irresistible.

4 ripe beefsteak tomatoes, thinly sliced • 14 ounces buffalo mozzarella, drained and torn into pieces • 4 handfuls of arugula leaves • 3 to 4 tablespoons fruity extra-virgin olive oil • salt and freshly ground black pepper

TO SERVE: focaccia bread

1 Lay the tomatoes on a large platter, overlapping the slices slightly. Arrange the mozzarella and arugula leaves attractively over the tomatoes.
2 Drizzle the olive oil over and season with salt and pepper. Serve the salad with slices of focaccia.

FIG & MOZZARELLA SALAD WITH WARM VINCOTTO DRESSING >

Fresh figs and mozzarella make a sublime combination, especially if you use a wonderful buffalo mozzarella. You should find vincotto vinegar at Italian markets or online, but if you cannot, balsamic vinegar works well, too.

6 ripe but firm figs, cut into quarters • 14 ounces buffalo mozzarella, drained and torn into pieces • 2 large handfuls of arugula leaves • 4 tablespoons extra-virgin olive oil • 1 to 2 tablespoons vincotto or balsamic vinegar • 1 small handful of red basil and parsley sprigs • salt and freshly ground black pepper

TO SERVE: olive ciabatta bread

1 Arrange the figs on a serving platter and top with the mozzarella. Scatter the arugula over the salad.
2 Gently warm the olive oil and vincotto in a small saucepan. Season with salt and pepper.
3 Drizzle the warm dressing over the salad and scatter the basil and parsley on top. Serve the salad with slices of olive ciabatta.

CHÈVRE TOASTS WITH CRANBERRY RELISH

Chèvre (goat cheese), broiled until melting, goes particularly well with a fruity cranberry relish.

12 slices of baguette • 1¼ pounds chèvre, cut into 12 slices • 2 tablespoons extra-virgin olive oil • freshly ground black pepper
CRANBERRY RELISH: 1 cup cranberry sauce • 1 small red onion, minced • finely grated zest and juice of 1 small orange, preferably a blood orange

TO SERVE: spinach, arugula and watercress salad

1 Preheat the broiler.
2 Lightly toast the baguette slices on one side under the broiler 1 to 2 minutes. Lay a slice of chèvre on the untoasted side. Drizzle a little olive oil over and season with pepper. Broil until the cheese has melted slightly, about 2 minutes.
3 Meanwhile, put the cranberry sauce in a bowl and stir in the onion and orange zest and juice.
4 Place three chèvre toasts on each serving plate and spoon the sauce around. Serve with a spinach, arugula and watercress salad.

PAN-FRIED HALLOUMI WITH QUICK TOMATO SAUCE

Halloumi could have been made for this dish, but if you have a favorite cheese that responds well to being pan-fried, then do use that instead. My local artisan cheesemaker produces a wonderful halloumi speckled with chili—it's hot and just delicious served this way.

3 tablespoons extra-virgin olive oil • 3 garlic cloves, roughly chopped • 14 ounces cherry tomatoes, cut in half • a splash of dry white wine or water • 8 small basil leaves • 1 pound 2 ounces halloumi cheese, patted dry and cut into 12 slices • salt and freshly ground black pepper

TO SERVE: green salad and crusty bread

1 Heat the olive oil in a large, nonstick frying pan or wok over high heat. Fry the garlic and tomatoes 3 minutes, squashing the tomatoes with the back of a fork from time to time.
2 Add the wine and basil, season with salt and pepper, and cook 1 minute longer.
3 Meanwhile, heat a large, nonstick frying pan or ridged grill pan over high heat. Fry or grill the halloumi slices, turning once, until softened and slightly golden in places, about 1 minute per side.
4 Serve the halloumi with the sauce alongside, and a salad of mixed greens and slices of crusty bread.

BLUE CHEESE, ENDIVE & WALNUT SALAD

Salty blue cheese, slightly bitter endive, crunchy celery and creamy walnuts are a match made in heaven. Gorgonzola is my own personal favorite in this salad, but do feel free to substitute your own preferred blue cheese.

2 heads of Belgian endive, trimmed and separated into leaves • 11 ounces strong blue cheese, such as Gorgonzola, Roquefort or Stilton, crumbled • 2 handfuls of walnut halves
DRESSING: 5 tablespoons extra-virgin olive oil • 2 tablespoons red wine vinegar • 1 teaspoon sugar • salt and freshly ground black pepper

TO SERVE: baguette

1 Arrange the endive leaves on a serving platter. Scatter the blue cheese and walnuts over.
2 Put all the ingredients for the dressing in a tightly capped jar, season with salt and pepper, and shake until emulsified. Pour the dressing over the salad, season with extra pepper, to taste, and serve with slices of baguette.

RICOTTA & TOMATO BRUSCHETTA

Make sure you use ripe, flavorsome tomatoes and fresh ricotta to top these bruschetta, and the results will be sublime.

12 slices of ciabatta bread • 4 large, vine-ripened tomatoes, roughly chopped • 1 garlic clove, roughly chopped • 4 tablespoons extra-virgin olive oil • 5 basil leaves, roughly torn • 1 pound 2 ounces fresh ricotta, sliced • salt and freshly ground black pepper

TO SERVE: arugula salad

1 Preheat the broiler, then toast both sides of the slices of ciabatta until light golden.
2 Meanwhile, put the tomatoes in a bowl. Stir in the garlic and 3 tablespoons of the olive oil. Add the basil and season with salt and pepper.
3 Place three slices of toast on each serving plate and pile the tomato mixture on top. Set a slice of ricotta on each, then drizzle the remaining olive oil over. Add a grinding of black pepper before serving with an arugula salad.

GARLIC MUSHROOMS ON ROSEMARY BRUSCHETTA >

Richly flavored mushrooms spiked with garlic and served on slices of crisp, rosemary-infused bruschetta… heavenly!

3 tablespoons extra-virgin olive oil • 2 garlic cloves, minced • 2 pounds cremini mushrooms • 1 small handful of parsley, leaves chopped • 1 small handful of red basil leaves • salt and freshly ground black pepper
ROSEMARY BRUSCHETTA: 12 thick slices of poppyseed bread • 4 to 5 tablespoons extra-virgin olive oil • 4 large rosemary sprigs

TO SERVE: mixed leaf salad

1 Preheat the broiler.
2 Heat the olive oil in a wok or large, nonstick frying pan over high heat. Stir-fry the garlic and mushrooms until the mushrooms are cooked and start to exude liquid, 3 to 4 minutes. Stir in the parsley and season with salt and pepper.
3 Meanwhile, toast both sides of the bread. Drizzle the olive oil over and rub with the rosemary, then season with salt. Serve the mushrooms on top of the bruschetta. Spoon any pan juices over and sprinkle with red basil. Serve with a mixed leaf salad.

CAPER & LEMON-BUTTER LINGUINE

1 pound 2 ounces fresh linguine, spaghetti or tagliatelle • 1 stick butter • juice of ½ lemon and strips of lemon zest • a pinch of sugar • 2 tablespoons salted capers, rinsed and drained • 1 small handful of baby parsley leaves • salt and freshly ground black pepper

TO SERVE: green salad

1 Bring a large saucepan of salted water to a boil and cook the linguine until al dente, about 2 minutes.
2 Meanwhile, melt the butter in a small pan over low heat, then stir in the lemon juice, sugar and capers. Season with salt and pepper. Keep warm.
3 Drain the pasta and toss with the lemon butter before serving sprinkled with the lemon zest and parsley. Serve with a salad of mixed greens.

QUICK CHILI NOODLES

Instant noodles are an absolute gift for the busy cook. Peanuts lend a gorgeous crunch and a great flavor to this family favorite—and, of course, they add valuable protein, too.

2 teaspoons vegetable bouillon powder • 9 ounces instant noodles • 6 tablespoons olive oil • 3 handfuls of sugar snap peas • a pinch of dried chili flakes • 1 garlic clove, halved • 2 to 3 tablespoons soy sauce • 1¼ cups roasted peanuts, coarsely crushed

1 Bring 2½ cups of water to a boil in a large saucepan. Stir in the bouillon powder and return to a boil.
2 Add the noodles, stir and cook until soft, 2 to 3 minutes.
3 Meanwhile, heat the olive oil in a wok or large, nonstick frying pan over medium heat. Add the sugar snap peas, chili flakes and garlic and stir-fry 1 minute. Remove the garlic.
4 Drain the noodles, then add them to the wok and pour in the soy sauce. Toss well until combined. Serve sprinkled with the crushed peanuts.

BEST BEANS ON TOAST

This makes a filling and fast dinner—it's one of my youngest son's favorite quick meals.

14 ounces canned cannellini beans, drained and rinsed • 3 garlic cloves, minced • 5 tablespoons fruity extra-virgin olive oil • 1 handful of parsley, leaves chopped • 8 slices of country-style bread • salt and freshly ground black pepper

TO SERVE: green salad

1 Put the beans in a saucepan with the garlic and 3 tablespoons of the olive oil. Cook over medium heat, stirring occasionally, until softened, 3 to 4 minutes. Stir in the parsley and season with salt and pepper.
2 Meanwhile, toast the bread. Spoon a little oil over the toast and top with the beans. Drizzle the remaining oil over the beans and serve with a salad of mixed greens.

IT'S HARD TO IMAGINE SITTING DOWN TO A FRAGRANT, CREAMY SHRIMP LAKSA, OR A STEAMING BOWL OF CHICKPEA, BACON & SPINACH STEW THAT HAS TAKEN JUST TEN MINUTES TO MAKE FROM BEGINNING TO BOWL. BUT WITH THE FOLLOWING RECIPES, AN AMAZING ARRAY OF FLAVORSOME FRESH MEALS CAN BE MADE IN NEXT TO NO TIME .

CHICKEN & BASIL STIR-FRY

Stir-frying is more often associated with Asian ingredients, but this simple Italian-style dish of chicken, tomatoes, olives and fresh basil works really well when cooked in a wok.

14 ounces dried orzo pasta • 1¼ pounds skinless, boneless chicken breast, cut in strips • 2 tablespoons olive oil • 11 ounces cherry tomatoes, cut in half • 1 handful of pitted black olives • 1 handful of basil leaves • juice of ½ lemon, or to taste • ¼ stick butter • salt and freshly ground black pepper

TO SERVE: green salad

1 Bring a large saucepan of salted water to a boil and cook the orzo until al dente, 5 to 6 minutes.
2 Meanwhile, season the chicken with salt and pepper. Heat the olive oil in a wok or large, nonstick frying pan over high heat. Stir-fry the chicken until it begins to turn golden, 4 to 5 minutes.
3 Add the tomatoes and olives, and stir-fry 3 minutes longer until the chicken is cooked. Stir in the basil and lemon juice, then adjust the seasoning to taste.
4 Drain the orzo, toss with the butter until coated, and serve with the chicken mixture and a salad of mixed greens.

COCONUT TURKEY STIR-FRY

Rice noodles make the perfect addition to this simple stir-fry, soaking up the spicy, creamy coconut sauce.

11 ounces thin rice stick noodles • 3 tablespoons olive oil • 1¼ pounds skinless, boneless turkey breast, cut in strips • ⅔ cup canned coconut cream • 1 teaspoon vegetable bouillon powder • 1 tablespoon red or green Thai curry paste • 3 handfuls of snow peas • 1 handful of cilantro, leaves chopped

1 Place the noodles in a heatproof bowl and cover with boiling water. Stir, cover and set aside until soft, about 3 minutes, then drain.
2 Meanwhile, heat the olive oil in a wok or large, nonstick frying pan over high heat. Stir-fry the turkey until light golden, about 4 to 5 minutes.
3 Add the coconut cream, vegetable bouillon powder and curry paste and stir well. Bring to a boil, then turn the heat down and simmer 1 minute.
4 Add the noodles and snow peas and stir to combine, then continue cooking until the turkey is cooked through and the sauce has thickened slightly, about 2 minutes. Add a little water if the sauce seems too dry. Stir in the cilantro and serve.

SPAGHETTI CARBONARA

The Sardinian ewe's milk cheese, pecorino sardo, is traditionally used in an authentic carbonara, but pre-grated Parmesan makes a good substitute for cooks in a hurry.

6 eggs • 1 cup grated Parmesan cheese, plus extra for serving • 1 tablespoon olive oil • 7 ounces pancetta or bacon, cut into cubes or strips • 2 garlic cloves, sliced • 1 pound 2 ounces fresh spaghetti • salt and freshly ground black pepper

TO SERVE: green salad

1 Beat the eggs and Parmesan together and season with salt and plenty of pepper.
2 Heat the olive oil in a large, nonstick frying pan over medium heat. Fry the pancetta with the garlic until the pancetta is golden, 4 to 5 minutes.
3 Meanwhile, bring a large saucepan of salted water to a boil and cook the spaghetti until al dente, about 2 minutes. Drain the pasta.
4 Return the pasta to the saucepan and, while it is still hot, add the pancetta and egg mixture and stir until combined. The pasta should be hot enough to cook the egg lightly; if it isn't, set the pan over low heat for a few seconds—any longer and the eggs will scramble.
5 Serve the pasta with extra Parmesan at the table and a salad of mixed greens.

CHICKPEA, BACON & SPINACH STEW

Canned cherry tomatoes make a great pantry standby and add a lovely texture as well as flavor to sauces, soups and stews. If you cannot find them, quartered whole canned tomatoes will work just as well.

3 tablespoons olive oil • 2 garlic cloves, minced • 7 ounces bacon, cut into cubes or strips • 2½ cups hot vegetable stock • 14 ounces canned cherry tomatoes, drained • 28 ounces canned chickpeas, drained and rinsed • 3 large handfuls of baby spinach leaves • salt and freshly ground black pepper

1 Heat the olive oil in a large saucepan over medium-high heat. Fry the garlic and bacon, stirring, until the bacon begins to turn crisp, about 3 minutes.
2 Add the vegetable stock, cherry tomatoes and chickpeas. Bring to a boil, then turn the heat down and simmer, stirring occasionally, until the stock has reduced slightly, 2 to 3 minutes.
3 Stir in the spinach and cook until just wilted, about 1 minute. Season with salt and pepper, then serve.

GARLIC & GINGER PORK

Garlic and ginger are sublime with pork. Add a little honey and a squeeze of lime, and the taste just gets better and better.

1 garlic clove, minced • 1 teaspoon ginger paste • 1¼ pounds lean boneless pork, cut in strips • 2 tablespoons olive oil • 2 tablespoons honey • juice of 1 lime • 2 teaspoons fish sauce • 1 handful of cilantro, chopped • 9 ounces dried egg noodles • 1 tablespoon toasted sesame oil • salt and freshly ground black pepper

1 Mix the garlic and ginger paste together and rub into the pork, then season with salt and pepper.
2 Heat the olive oil in a wok or large, nonstick frying pan over high heat. Stir-fry the pork until cooked, about 5 minutes. Stir in the honey, lime juice and fish sauce and cook, stirring regularly, until the pork is golden and glossy, about 1 minute. Add the cilantro.
3 Meanwhile, bring a large pan of salted water to a boil and cook the noodles until soft, 3 to 4 minutes. Drain, then toss the noodles with the sesame oil and serve with the pork.

SPICY BEEF IN LETTUCE CUPS >

Kecap manis should be easy to find in large supermarkets or Asian markets, but if you have difficulty sourcing it, simply use dark soy sauce and add an extra tablespoon of dark brown sugar.

3 tablespoons olive oil • 1 onion, chopped • 2 garlic cloves, sliced • 1 pound lean ground steak • ⅓ cup kecap manis (Indonesian sweet soy sauce) • ½ teaspoon dried chili flakes • 1 teaspoon ginger paste • 2 tablespoons dark brown sugar • 2 tablespoons ketchup • 1 handful of cilantro, leaves chopped • 8 large iceberg lettuce leaves

TO SERVE: naan breads

1 Heat the olive oil in a wok or large, nonstick frying pan over high heat. Stir-fry the onion and garlic 30 seconds. Add the beef and stir-fry until browned, about 5 minutes.
2 Stir in the kecap manis, chili flakes, ginger paste, sugar and ketchup. Cook 2 minutes longer, then stir in the cilantro.
3 To serve, spoon the beef mixture into the lettuce cups and serve with the naan breads.

CARIBBEAN BLACKENED BEEF WITH MANGO MAYONNAISE

I love to serve this Caribbean-style beef with peshwari naan, because it reminds me of the wonderful coconut roti bread found in the West Indies. Plain naan bread is a good alternative, if you can't find the peshwari.

6 tablespoons olive oil • 2 shallots, peeled • 1 garlic clove, peeled • 1 teaspoon ground allspice • a pinch of ground nutmeg • a pinch of ground cinnamon • 1 teaspoon dried thyme • a pinch of dried chili flakes • 1 tablespoon dark brown sugar • 2 tablespoons dark rum • 1 pound lean boneless beef, cut in strips • ⅔ cup mayonnaise • 2 tablespoons mango chutney

TO SERVE: peshwari naan breads and green salad

1 Pour 4 tablespoons of the olive oil into a food processor or blender and add the shallots, garlic, spices, thyme, chili flakes, brown sugar and rum. Blitz everything to a paste, then transfer the mixture to a bowl and add the beef. Turn the beef until it is coated in the marinade.
2 Heat the remaining oil in a wok or large, nonstick frying pan over high heat. Stir-fry the beef until cooked, 3 to 4 minutes.
3 Mix the mayonnaise and mango chutney together. Serve the beef with the mango mayonnaise, naan breads and a salad of mixed greens.

LEMON & BASIL VEAL CUTLETS >

This simple but stunning dish uses boneless slices of veal called cutlets or scallops.

4 thin veal cutlets, each about 6 ounces • 2 tablespoons olive oil • 2 garlic cloves, thinly sliced • 1 handful of basil leaves • juice of 1 lemon • salt and freshly ground black pepper

TO SERVE: lemon wedges, crusty bread and herb salad

1 Season the veal with salt and pepper. Heat the olive oil in a large, nonstick frying pan over high heat. Fry the veal, turning once, until golden in places, about 2 minutes per side.
2 Turn the heat down and add the garlic and basil, then cook 1 minute longer. Remove the pan momentarily from the heat and squeeze in the lemon juice.
3 Return the pan to the heat and bubble until the cutlets are golden, about 2 minutes.
4 Serve the veal, spooning any pan juices over the meat, with lemon wedges, slices of bread and a herb salad.

BROILED SARDINES ON BRUSCHETTA

This is rather elegant and makes a delicious, nutritious light meal served with a salad.

16 fresh sardine fillets • 2 tablespoons olive oil, plus extra for drizzling • juice of 1 lemon • 4 large slices of country-style wholegrain bread • 1 garlic clove, cut in half • 2 thyme sprigs • salt and freshly ground black pepper

TO SERVE: lemon wedges and tomato salad

1 Preheat the broiler.
2 Season the sardines with salt and pepper and place skin-side up in the broiler pan. Drizzle a little of the olive oil over them and add a squeeze of lemon juice. Broil the sardines about 3 inches from the heat until cooked through, 3 to 4 minutes.
3 Meanwhile, heat a ridged grill pan over high heat. Toast the bread on the grill pan until blackened in places, about 1 minute per side. Rub the cut side of the garlic firmly over the toasted bread. Drizzle the remaining olive oil over, then rub on the thyme.
4 Top each slice of bread with four sardine fillets and serve with lemon wedges and a tomato salad.

SEARED SALMON WITH CUCUMBER RELISH

This makes great everyday eating but is good enough to serve for a special dinner, too. For a deliciously different accompaniment, I've suggested giant couscous—its nutty, pearly grains take only minutes to cook—but you can use regular couscous instead.

1⅓ cups giant couscous • juice of 1 large lemon • 4 tablespoons olive oil • 1 small handful of parsley, leaves chopped • 4 skinless salmon fillets, each about 6 ounces • 1 large hothouse cucumber, peeled, seeded and diced • 1 handful of mint, leaves minced • ½ teaspoon sugar • 4 tablespoons white wine vinegar • salt and freshly ground black pepper

1 Cook the couscous in a saucepan of boiling salted water until tender, 6 to 8 minutes. Drain and stir in half the lemon juice, half the olive oil and the parsley. Set aside.
2 While the couscous is cooking, season the salmon fillets with salt and pepper. Heat the remaining oil in a large, nonstick frying pan over medium-high heat and fry the salmon, turning once, until cooked but still slightly opaque in the center, 3 to 4 minutes per side.
3 Meanwhile, make the cucumber relish: Put the cucumber in a bowl and stir in the mint, sugar and white wine vinegar; season to taste.
4 Squeeze the remaining lemon juice liberally over the cooked salmon and serve with the cucumber relish and giant couscous.

PAN-GRILLED SMOKED SALMON WRAPS

These are great for a simple midweek meal, served with a salad of mixed greens.

9 ounces cream cheese • 4 large flour tortillas • 6 scallions, minced • 9 ounces sliced smoked salmon • 8 sun-dried tomatoes in olive oil, drained and chopped • 1 small handful of dill, stalks discarded • 2 tablespoons olive oil

TO SERVE: green salad

1 Spread the cream cheese over the flour tortillas, then scatter the scallions on top. Lay the salmon slices evenly over each tortilla and top with the sun-dried tomatoes and dill leaves.
2 Fold in the sides of each tortilla, then roll up to form a long sausage shape. Cut each tortilla roll in half diagonally.
3 Heat a ridged grill pan over medium heat. Cook the wraps, turning once, until heated though, 2 to 3 minutes. (You may need to cook them in two batches.) Serve hot with a salad of mixed greens.

TUNA & CHERRY TOMATO SPIEDINI

Spiedini is the Italian word for skewers of meat or fish that are cooked on a barbecue, under the broiler or, as here, pan-grilled. You will need 8 metal skewers.

juice of 1 lemon • 1 pound tuna loin, cut into 24 bite-size pieces • 11 ounces cherry tomatoes • 6 tablespoons olive oil • 4 large handfuls of mixed salad greens • 1 avocado, pitted and sliced • 2 tablespoons mixed toasted seeds • 2 tablespoons balsamic vinegar • salt and freshly ground black pepper

TO SERVE: ciabatta bread

1 Squeeze the lemon juice over the tuna and season with salt and pepper. Divide the tuna equally among the skewers, alternating each piece with a cherry tomato.
2 Heat 2 tablespoons of the olive oil in a ridged grill pan over high heat. Grill the skewers, turning often, until the tuna is golden on the outside and the tomatoes are slightly blistered and softened, 3 to 4 minutes.
3 Meanwhile, put the salad greens in a large bowl and add the avocado and seeds. Pour in the remaining olive oil and the balsamic vinegar, then toss until combined. Serve two skewers per person with the salad and slices of ciabatta.

SHRIMP LAKSA >

This is one of my favorite quick meals because it doesn't require precise measurements and you can change the vegetables, or even add extra, according to what you have on hand. Look for laksa paste in Asian markets or online.

11 ounces thin rice stick noodles • 1¾ cups canned coconut milk • 1¾ cups chicken stock • 2 tablespoons laksa paste • 1 handful of cherry tomatoes, cut in half • 1 handful of sugar snap peas • 1 pound cooked, peeled (but tail on) extra-large or large shrimp • 1 small bunch of cilantro, leaves roughly chopped

1 Place the noodles in a heatproof bowl and cover with boiling water. Stir, cover and set aside until soft, about 3 minutes, then drain.
2 Meanwhile, pour the coconut milk and stock into a saucepan, stir in the laksa paste and cook 5 minutes over medium heat, stirring occasionally.
3 Stir in the tomatoes, sugar snap peas, shrimp and noodles and cook until heated through, about 2 minutes. Stir in the cilantro and serve.

SIZZLED SQUID WITH LIME & CILANTRO DRESSING

I have to admit to cooking more than the stated quantities here—I have a serious addiction to crisp, golden baby squid drenched in lime!

3 tablespoons all-purpose flour • 1 pound cleaned and prepared squid (calamari), sliced • ½ cup extra-virgin olive oil • juice of 1 lime • pinch of sugar • 1 tablespoon chopped cilantro leaves • salt and freshly ground black pepper

TO SERVE: seeded bread and arugula salad

1 Put the flour in a bowl and season with salt and pepper. Dip the squid in the seasoned flour to coat.
2 Heat 2 tablespoons of the olive oil in a large, nonstick frying pan over high heat. Fry the squid until crisp and golden, about 3 minutes. Drain the squid on paper towels.
3 While the squid is cooking, pour the remaining olive oil into a small pan and add the lime juice, sugar and cilantro. Season to taste and heat gently.
4 Drizzle the warm dressing over and serve with bread and an arugula salad.

CRISP-CRUMBED SQUID WITH AÏOLI

I love squid coated in crisp golden crumbs even more than I like the battered version that is typically found in many Mediterranean countries. For the aïoli, choose a good-quality mayonnaise.

12 medium, cleaned and prepared squid (calamari), cut into 2-inch pieces, and tentacles reserved • 6 tablespoons dry white bread crumbs • 1 egg white, lightly whisked with a fork • 4 tablespoons olive oil • salt and freshly ground black pepper
AÏOLI: ⅔ cup mayonnaise • 2 garlic cloves, minced • juice of ½ lemon

TO SERVE: lemon wedges, green salad and baguette

1 Score a diamond pattern lightly across the pieces of squid using the tip of a sharp knife.
2 Scatter the bread crumbs over a large plate and season with salt and pepper. Dip the squid, including the tentacles, briefly into the egg white and shake to remove any excess, then lightly coat in the bread crumbs.
3 Heat the olive oil in a large, nonstick frying pan over high heat. Fry the squid until crisp and golden, about 1 minute per side. (You may need to cook it in two batches.)
4 Meanwhile, mix the mayonnaise with the garlic and lemon juice. Serve the squid with the aïoli, lemon wedges, a salad of mixed greens and slices of baguette.

SPICED LEMON SCALLOPS

Buy the plumpest scallops you can find and you will adore this dish. The lightly spiced scallops are pan-grilled and served with a warm lentil salad. If you can't find vacuum-packed lentils, you can use canned, but rinse and drain them well.

2 teaspoons Thai red curry paste • 1 teaspoon sugar • juice of 1 lemon • 6 tablespoons olive oil • 16 fresh sea scallops • 2½ cups pre-cooked vacuum-packed lentils • 1 small handful of cilantro, leaves chopped

TO SERVE: spinach salad

1 Mix together the Thai curry paste, sugar and half the lemon juice with 2 tablespoons of the olive oil. Brush the mixture all over the scallops.
2 Pour any remaining spice mixture into a small saucepan, add another tablespoon of the oil and warm over low heat.
3 Meanwhile, put the cooked lentils in a pan with 2 tablespoons of the oil and the remaining lemon juice and heat 2 to 3 minutes; keep warm.
4 Heat the remaining oil in a ridged grill pan over very high heat. Grill the scallops until golden on the outside but still juicy and opaque in the center, about 1 minute per side.
5 Divide the lentils among four plates and top with the scallops. Spoon a little of the spiced dressing around them. Sprinkle with cilantro and serve with a spinach leaf salad.

SCRAMBLED EGGS WITH ASPARAGUS

This is a classic and for very good reason. It's certainly a "must-enjoy" during the season for locally grown asparagus.

9 ounces trimmed asparagus, cut into 1-inch pieces • 10 extra-large eggs, lightly beaten • 4 tablespoons heavy cream (optional) • ¼ stick butter • 8 slices of country-style bread • salt and freshly ground black pepper

1 Bring a saucepan of water to a boil, then drop in the asparagus and blanch until al dente, about 1 minute. Drain and keep warm.
2 Meanwhile, season the eggs with salt and pepper and stir in the cream, if using.
3 Melt half the butter in a heavy-based, nonstick saucepan over medium heat. Pour in the eggs and cook, stirring constantly, until the eggs are lightly set but still moist, about 3 minutes.
4 At the same time, toast the bread. Spread the toast with the remaining butter.
5 Stir two-thirds of the asparagus into the eggs. Top the slices of toast with the scrambled egg and the remaining asparagus, then serve.

EGGS FLORENTINE >

Crisp toast topped with lemony spinach and a golden, runny egg makes heavenly eating for something so simple and speedy.

½ stick butter • 4 large handfuls of baby spinach leaves • juice of ½ lemon • splash of white wine vinegar • 4 extra-large eggs • 4 thick slices of country-style bread • salt and freshly ground black pepper

1 Melt half the butter in a large, nonstick frying pan over medium heat. Add the spinach and cook, stirring regularly, until wilted, about 3 minutes. Season to taste with salt and pepper and the lemon juice.
2 Meanwhile, pour enough water into a shallow saucepan or deep frying pan to come half way up the sides. Heat to just below boiling point and add the white wine vinegar. Carefully break in the eggs and poach over low heat until just set, about 2 minutes.
3 While the eggs are cooking, toast the bread and spread with the remaining butter. Top each slice of toast with some spinach and a poached egg. Add a grinding of black pepper and serve.

MINTED COUSCOUS & FETA SALAD >

This is a wonderfully quick and delicious vegetarian main meal.

1⅔ cups couscous • 2 cups hot vegetable stock • 1 small hothouse cucumber, diced • 4 ripe tomatoes, roughly chopped • 1 bunch of scallions, chopped • 1 large handful of pitted black olives • 1 handful of mint, leaves roughly torn • 9 ounces feta cheese, crumbled • salt and freshly ground black pepper

1 Put the couscous in a bowl and pour the hot stock over to cover. Stir, then cover and set aside until the stock is absorbed, 4 to 5 minutes. Fluff up the grains using a fork.
2 Stir the cucumber, tomatoes, scallions, olives and mint into the couscous, then season with salt and pepper. Add the feta and toss gently until everything is evenly combined.

CHILI-FRIED EGGS WITH TOMATO TOASTS

Frying the eggs in chili oil adds a little extra oomph, while rubbing the toast with fresh tomato is a simple way of adding a new dimension to toasted bread.

6 tablespoons olive oil • 1 to 2 small dried chilies (mildly hot or hot, to taste) • 4 extra-large eggs • 4 thick slices of country-style bread • 2 ripe tomatoes, cut in half • salt and freshly ground black pepper

TO SERVE: watercress and spinach salad

1 Heat the olive oil in a large, nonstick frying pan over medium heat. Crumble in the chilies, then carefully break the eggs into the pan. Fry the eggs, occasionally spooning the oil over, until the whites are set but the yolks remain runny, 2 to 3 minutes.
2 Meanwhile, toast the bread. Rub the cut surface of the tomatoes over one side of each slice of toast and season with salt and pepper
3 Top the toast with the fried eggs and drizzle a little of the chili oil from the pan over. Serve with a watercress and spinach salad.

GRILLED HALLOUMI, PISTACHIO & WATERMELON SALAD

The salty-sweet/crunchy-soft combination of pan-grilled halloumi, watermelon and pistachios is absolutely stunning. Plenty of freshly ground black pepper is a must.

½ small watermelon, seeded, and cut into bite-size chunks • 2 handfuls of unsalted shelled pistachios • 1 pound 2 ounces halloumi cheese, patted dry and diced • juice of ½ to 1 lime • 1 small handful of mint leaves • freshly ground black pepper

TO SERVE: lime wedges, pita breads and green salad

1 Put the watermelon on a large platter and scatter the pistachios over.

2 Heat a ridged grill pan over high heat. Grill the halloumi, turning often, until golden on all sides, about 2 minutes in total. Scatter the halloumi over the watermelon and squeeze lime juice to taste over the cheese.

3 Top with the mint leaves and season with pepper. Serve while the cheese is still warm with lime wedges, pita breads and a crisp green salad.

ROQUEFORT, ARUGULA & PITA SALAD

Roquefort is sublime in this salad, but any gutsy blue cheese can be used as a substitute.

2 tablespoons extra-virgin olive oil • 2 pita breads, torn into bite-size pieces • 2 garlic cloves, peeled • 4 handfuls of arugula • 9 ounces Roquefort cheese, crumbled into bite-size pieces • 3 celery stalks, thinly sliced diagonally • 6 moist dried figs, roughly chopped • 1 handful of chopped toasted hazelnuts
DRESSING: 6 tablespoons extra-virgin olive oil • 3 tablespoons balsamic vinegar • 1 garlic clove, minced • salt and freshly ground black pepper

1 Heat the olive oil in a large, nonstick frying pan over medium heat. Fry the pieces of pita with the garlic, turning occasionally, until the bread is golden, about 2 minutes. Remove the pita from the pan, season with salt and pepper and set aside. Discard the garlic.
2 Put the arugula in a salad bowl and scatter the Roquefort over. Next, add the celery, figs, hazelnuts and fried pita bread.
3 Put all the ingredients for the dressing into a tightly capped jar and shake until emulsified. Season to taste. Pour the dressing over the salad, toss gently until combined, then serve.

PEACH & FETA SALAD WITH LIME DRESSING

This salad is full of fresh, summery flavors, and the combination of fruit, vegetables, cheese and lentils makes a well-balanced meal. You could also try ready-cooked quinoa in place of lentils.

4 handfuls of fine green beans, trimmed • 2½ cups pre-cooked vacuum-packed (or canned, drained and rinsed) green or brown lentils • 4 firm but ripe peaches, cut in half, pitted and sliced • 9 ounces jarred, marinated artichoke hearts, drained • 1 pound feta cheese, crumbled into bite-size pieces • 1 handful of unsalted shelled pistachios • 1 handful of mint leaves
DRESSING: 6 tablespoons extra-virgin olive oil • juice of 1 lime • ½ teaspoon sugar • salt and freshly ground black pepper

1 Bring a saucepan of water to a boil and drop in the beans. Blanch until crisp-tender, about 2 minutes, then drain and transfer to a salad bowl.
2 Add the lentils to the bowl along with the peaches, artichokes, feta, pistachios and mint.
3 Put all the ingredients for the dressing into a tightly capped jar and shake until emulsified. Season to taste. Pour the dressing over the salad and toss gently until combined, then serve.

SPAGHETTINI WITH CHILI OIL & GARLIC

Spaghettini is slightly finer than spaghetti so cooks in less time. You could use fresh pasta if you have trouble finding spaghettini.

1 pound dried spaghettini • 6 tablespoons olive oil • 1 small dried chili (mildly hot or hot, to taste) • 1 garlic clove, cut in half • ½ cup grated Parmesan cheese, for serving • salt

TO SERVE: peppery green salad

1 Bring a large saucepan of salted water to a boil and cook the spaghettini until al dente, 7 to 8 minutes.
2 Meanwhile, pour the olive oil into a large, nonstick frying pan and crumble in the dried chili. Add the garlic and heat gently until the oil is warm and infused with the flavors of the garlic and chili, 3 to 4 minutes. Discard the garlic.
3 Using pasta tongs, lift the pasta from the cooking water into the pan with the garlic oil and toss well until coated. Sprinkle Parmesan on top and serve with a salad of peppery greens.

PARMESAN, SAGE & PEPPERCORN PASTA >

Parmesan adds a delicious flavor here, but I also love Sicilian ricotta salata grated over this simple dish—the sheep milk cheese has a little more kick than Parmesan, so if you come across it, give it a try.

1 pound 2 ounces fresh penne pasta • ¼ stick butter • 2 garlic cloves, thinly sliced • 1 handful of sage leaves • 1 teaspoon pink or green peppercorns in brine, drained and crushed • ½ cup grated Parmesan cheese (or ricotta salata) • a few sprigs of flat-leaf parsley • salt

TO SERVE: mixed leaf salad

1 Bring a large saucepan of salted water to a boil and cook the penne until al dente, about 2 minutes.
2 Meanwhile, melt the butter in a small pan over low heat. Add the garlic and sage. Remove from the heat and set aside to let the flavors infuse while the pasta cooks.
3 Drain the pasta and return it to the pan. Pour the sage butter over and toss well until coated. Stir in the peppercorns. Sprinkle with the Parmesan, scatter the parsley over and serve with a mixed leaf salad.

CHILI HOISIN NOODLES WITH TOFU

I often serve this one-bowl meal as a quick weekday dinner. Tofu, which is made from soybeans, is a great source of protein and calcium. It has the ability to absorb flavors well, so the combination of ginger, chili and hoisin sauce creates a really tasty, healthy dish.

9 ounces dried egg noodles • 1 pound 2 ounces firm tofu, patted dry and cut into cubes • 1 tablespoon toasted sesame oil • 4 tablespoons peanut or sunflower oil • 2-inch piece fresh ginger root, peeled and shredded • 2 garlic cloves, sliced • 1 bunch of scallions, chopped • 4 handfuls of watercress • ½ to 1 teaspoon dried chili flakes • 2 tablespoons hoisin sauce • 3 tablespoons vegetable stock or water

1 Bring a large saucepan of salted water to a boil and cook the noodles until just softened, 2 to 3 minutes. Drain and rinse under cold running water, then toss with the sesame oil.
2 Meanwhile, heat 2 tablespoons of the peanut oil in a large, nonstick frying pan over high heat. Fry the tofu until golden, about 3 minutes; keep warm.
3 Heat the remaining peanut oil in a wok or large, nonstick frying pan over medium-high heat. Stir-fry the ginger and garlic 30 seconds.
4 Add half the scallions, the watercress, chili flakes and cooked noodles. Stir-fry 2 minutes, then add the hoisin sauce and stock. Toss well until combined and heated through.
5 Serve the noodles topped with the tofu and remaining scallions.

ARUGULA & PARMESAN PENNE

This simple pasta dish makes a great summer meal. For a delicious variation, you could try adding a little ricotta just before the arugula.

1 pound 2 ounces fresh penne pasta • 3 tablespoons olive oil • 2 handfuls of arugula • 1 cup grated Parmesan cheese • finely grated zest of 1 lemon (optional) • salt and freshly ground black pepper

TO SERVE: tomato salad

1 Bring a large saucepan of salted water to a boil and cook the penne until al dente, about 2 minutes. Drain the pasta and return it to the pan.
2 Stir in the olive oil, arugula, Parmesan and lemon zest, if using. Season with pepper. Return to the heat 1 minute or so until the arugula has wilted. Serve with a tomato salad.

OPEN RICOTTA LASAGNE

This dish shows that there really is no need to go to elaborate lengths making sauces when you're pushed for time. All it takes is a handful of good, simple ingredients and a little imagination.

12 (4-inch) squares of fresh lasagne • 1¼ pounds vine-ripened tomatoes, seeded and roughly chopped • 4 tablespoons extra-virgin olive oil • 1 handful of basil leaves, plus extra for garnish • 1 pound fresh ricotta • salt and freshly ground black pepper

TO SERVE: arugula salad

1 Bring a large saucepan of salted water to a boil and cook the lasagne until al dente, 2 to 3 minutes, then drain.
2 Meanwhile, put the tomatoes in a bowl and stir in the olive oil and basil. Season with salt and pepper, then set aside.
3 Place a sheet of lasagne on each of four plates and top with a big spoonful of the tomato mixture. Add a second sheet of lasagne. Dot three-fourths of the ricotta over the pasta and cover with another sheet of lasagne. Add another layer of tomatoes, then top with the remaining ricotta.
4 Drizzle the juices from the tomatoes over and around the lasagne and season generously with pepper. Garnish with a few extra basil leaves and serve with an arugula salad.

PIADINA PIZZA MARGARITA

Piadine are Italian flatbreads that are very similar to flour tortillas, so if you can't find the authentic version, simply use tortillas instead.

8 small piadine (or flour tortillas) • ½ cup tomato purée • 1 teaspoon dried oregano • 7 ounces buffalo mozzarella, drained and torn into pieces • 1 to 2 tablespoons olive oil • 8 to 10 basil leaves, roughly torn • salt and freshly ground black pepper

TO SERVE: Italian-style salad

1 Preheat the oven to 400°F.
2 Lay two piadine together, one on top of the other, to make four pizza bases. Place them on two baking sheets. Mix the tomato purée and oregano together and spread evenly over the pizza bases.
3 Arrange the mozzarella on the sauce. Drizzle some olive oil over and season with salt and pepper. Scatter the basil on top. Bake until the mozzarella has melted and is starting to color, about 5 minutes. Serve with an Italian-style salad of mixed greens.

A HEALTHY SESAME CHICKEN SALAD, WHOLESOME AND HEARTY SPICED SALMON IN NOODLE MISO BROTH, AND EXOTIC GOLDEN GINGER DUCK ARE JUST SOME OF THE DELECTABLE DISHES IN THIS CHAPTER. NOT ONLY ARE THEY A BREEZE TO PREPARE, THEY'RE ALSO BURSTING WITH GOODNESS AND FLAVOR. GREAT-TASTING FOOD NEEDN'T TAKE AN AGE TO MAKE!

FIFTEEN-MINUTE MEALS

HOT CHICKEN STICKS WITH GUACAMOLE >

To speed up cooking, buy ready-sliced chicken breasts, if you can. Chili fans might like to add a splash of chili oil to the guacamole and diced tomato and chopped cilantro also make great additions. You will need 12 metal skewers.

1¼ pounds skinless, boneless chicken breast, cut in strips • 2 tablespoons olive oil • 2 tablespoons chopped cilantro leaves • salt and freshly ground black pepper
GUACAMOLE: 2 ripe avocados, pitted • 1 garlic clove, minced • juice of 1 lime • 2 tablespoons extra-virgin olive oil • grated zest of 1 lime

TO SERVE: tortillas, lime wedges and green salad

1 Thread the chicken onto 12 skewers in a concertina fashion. Brush with 1 tablespoon of the olive oil and season with salt and pepper.
2 Heat the remaining oil in a ridged grill pan over medium-high heat. Grill the skewers, turning occasionally, until cooked through and golden, 8 to 10 minutes.
3 Meanwhile, make the guacamole. Scoop out the avocado into a bowl and mash with the garlic. Stir in the lime juice and olive oil, then season to taste. Scatter half of the lime zest over the top.
4 Sprinkle the cilantro and remaining lime zest over the chicken sticks. Serve with the guacamole, tortillas, lime wedges and a salad of mixed greens.

CHICKEN & COCONUT SOUP

Coconut milk gives this soup a lovely richness, and when combined with chunky, Asian-style vegetables, it makes a hearty, satisfying dish —the perfect easy, complete meal in a bowl.

1¾ cups canned coconut milk • 2½ cups chicken stock • 6 scallions, sliced diagonally • 2 handfuls of baby corn • 9 ounces shredded cooked chicken breast • 1 carrot, shredded • 1 cup snow peas • 1 handful of cilantro, leaves chopped • salt and freshly ground black pepper

1 Pour the coconut milk and chicken stock into a large saucepan and bring to a boil. Turn the heat down, add the scallions and baby corn, and simmer 2 minutes.
2 Add the chicken, carrot, snow peas and cilantro, and season with salt and pepper. Warm through and serve hot.

SESAME CHICKEN SALAD

Sesame seeds make a crunchy, golden coating for strips of chicken. I also like to serve these as a finger food at parties, with a bowl of sweet chili sauce for dipping.

1 egg • ⅔ cup sesame seeds • 1 pound skinless, boneless chicken breast, cut in strips
• 3 tablespoons olive oil • 4 handfuls of bean sprouts • 1 small bunch of scallions, coarsely chopped • 2 carrots, cut into thin ribbons
• 9 ounces cherry tomatoes, cut in half
DRESSING: juice of 1 lime • 1 teaspoon honey
• 4 tablespoons olive oil

1 Beat the egg in a bowl and put the sesame seeds on a plate. Dip the strips of chicken into the egg and shake off any excess, then turn them in the sesame seeds until lightly coated.
2 Heat the olive oil in a wok or large, nonstick frying pan over high heat. Fry the chicken, turning once, until golden and cooked through, about 5 minutes. Drain on paper towels.
3 Meanwhile, put the bean sprouts, scallions, carrots and tomatoes in a serving bowl.
4 Mix the ingredients for the dressing together, pour it over the salad and toss until combined. Serve the salad topped with the chicken.

GOLDEN GINGER DUCK

Keep ginger fresh by storing it, already peeled, in the freezer. There's no need to thaw it before use—simply grate straight from frozen.

2½ cups vegetable or chicken stock
• 4 tablespoons orange marmalade • 1 garlic clove, minced • 1-inch piece fresh ginger root, peeled and grated • 3 tablespoons soy sauce
• 2 teaspoons fish sauce • 2 tablespoons salted peanuts, crushed (optional) • 4 skinless duck breasts, cut into thin strips • 9 ounces instant noodles • 3 tablespoons sunflower oil
• 1¼ pounds prepared stir-fry vegetables

1 Bring the stock to a boil in a large saucepan.
2 Meanwhile, put the marmalade in a bowl with the garlic, ginger, soy sauce and fish sauce. Add the peanuts, if using, and stir well. Dip the duck into the mixture and turn until well coated.
3 Add the noodles to the boiling stock and cook until soft, about 3 to 4 minutes, then drain.
4 While the noodles are cooking, heat 2 tablespoons of the sunflower oil in a wok or large, nonstick frying pan over medium-high heat. Stir-fry the vegetables until slightly softened, about 2 minutes, then remove them from the wok and keep warm.
5 Heat the remaining oil in the wok and stir-fry the duck until golden and just cooked (it should still be slightly pink in the center), 3 to 4 minutes. Serve the noodles topped with the vegetables and duck.

PANCETTA-WRAPPED CHEESE WITH SPINACH SALAD

Hot pancetta-wrapped cheese and peppery spinach make a great informal dinner with a glass of red wine.

1 pound provolone cheese, cut into 3- x 1-inch strips • 6 ounces thinly sliced pancetta or bacon • 2 tablespoons olive oil • 8 sun-dried tomatoes in olive oil • 4 large handfuls of baby spinach leaves • 2 tablespoons toasted pine nuts • 1 ripe but firm avocado, pitted and sliced • 1 tablespoon balsamic vinegar • salt and freshly ground black pepper

TO SERVE: olive ciabatta bread

1 Wrap each piece of provolone in a slice of pancetta. Heat the olive oil in a large, nonstick frying pan over high heat. Fry the pancetta-wrapped cheese until beginning to color and turn crisp, about 20 seconds per side. Drain on paper towels.
2 Meanwhile, drain the sun-dried tomatoes, reserving the oil, and cut them in half.
3 Place the spinach in a serving bowl and add the pine nuts, sun-dried tomatoes and avocado.
4 Whisk 4 tablespoons of the sun-dried tomato oil with the balsamic vinegar, then season with salt and pepper. Pour this dressing over the salad and toss well until coated.
5 Serve the pancetta-wrapped cheese on top of the salad, with slices of olive ciabatta on the side.

LIME & LEMONGRASS PORK

Choose lean ground pork, then keep the heat high and the meat moving during cooking, and you'll get golden pork that is slightly crisp.

2 tablespoons olive oil • 1 lemongrass stalk, peeled, crushed and minced • 1 onion, chopped • 2 garlic cloves, minced • 1 celery stalk, chopped • 1 pound lean ground pork • 2 handfuls of snow peas • 1 handful of baby corn • 9 ounces dried egg noodles • juice of 1 large lime • salt and freshly ground black pepper

1 Heat the olive oil in a wok or large, nonstick frying pan over high heat. Fry the lemongrass, onion, garlic, celery and ground pork, stirring regularly, until the pork is golden, about 8 minutes. Season with salt and pepper.
2 Add the snow peas and baby corn and continue stir-frying until the pork is cooked, about 2 minutes.
3 Meanwhile, bring a pan of salted water to a boil and cook the noodles until soft, 3 to 4 minutes. Drain well.
4 Stir the lime juice into the pork mixture and serve on top of the noodles.

MIGAS CON CHORIZO

Migas is the Spanish word for "crumbs" or "small pieces of bread" and, at its most basic, this traditional peasant dish consists of stale leftover bread simply fried in a little lard. However, each region has its own adaptation and this is my version.

2 tablespoons olive oil • 3 garlic cloves, sliced • 3 thick slices of country-style white bread, crusts removed and torn into bite-size pieces • 11 ounces Spanish chorizo picante, sliced into bite-size pieces • 1 cup jarred, roasted red bell peppers in olive oil, drained and sliced • 1 small bunch of flat-leaf parsley, leaves chopped • salt and freshly ground black pepper

TO SERVE: peppery mizuna salad

1 Heat the olive oil in a large, nonstick frying pan over low heat. Add the garlic and fry until the oil is infused with garlic flavor, about 2 minutes. Add the bread, turn the heat up a little, and fry until golden all over, 3 to 4 minutes.
2 Stir in the chorizo and cook, stirring frequently, until it is hot and sizzling, 3 to 4 minutes. Toss in the peppers and cook 1 minute longer. Season with salt and pepper, and scatter the parsley over. Serve with a mizuna salad.

LIMA BEAN & CHORIZO PAN-FRY >

Lima beans and piquant chorizo make great partners in this speedy dish, which needs nothing more than some good crusty bread and a green salad to make a satisfying and tasty meal.

3 tablespoons olive oil • 1 onion, minced • 28 ounces canned crushed tomatoes, drained • ½ teaspoon sugar • 28 ounces canned jumbo lima beans, drained and rinsed • 8 ounces Spanish chorizo, sliced or diced • a few flat-leaf parsley sprigs • salt and freshly ground black pepper

TO SERVE: green salad and crusty bread

1 Heat the oil in a large, nonstick frying pan over medium heat. Fry the onion, stirring regularly, until starting to soften, 2 to 3 minutes.
2 Add the tomatoes and sugar, and season with salt and pepper. Stir in the lima beans and chorizo. Bring to a boil, then turn the heat down and simmer until thickened, about 10 minutes.
3 Scatter the parsley over the top and serve with a crisp green salad and slices of crusty bread.

HERBY PORK SKEWERS

These tasty skewers are cooked in a grill pan, but they also make great barbecue food. Chicken is equally delicious prepared in this way. You will need 16 metal skewers.

4 thin, boneless pork steaks, each about 6 ounces, fat trimmed and each cut into 4 long strips • 4 tablespoons olive oil • 2 garlic cloves, minced • 2 tablespoons chopped rosemary leaves • finely grated zest and juice of 1 lemon • salt and freshly ground black pepper

TO SERVE: arugula salad and flatbreads

1 Thread the pork onto 16 skewers in a concertina fashion and place in a shallow dish.
2 Mix 3 tablespoons of the olive oil with the garlic, rosemary, and lemon zest and juice, then pour the mixture over the pork. Season with a little salt and pepper and turn until coated.
3 Heat the remaining oil in a ridged grill pan over high heat. Grill until the pork is cooked through, about 3 minutes per side. (You may need to cook the skewers in two batches.) Serve with an arugula salad and flatbreads.

< LAMB STEAKS WITH BLACKBERRY SAUCE

Tangy blackberry jam and rich, sweet balsamic vinegar are an unusual accompaniment for lamb, but the gorgeous fruity flavors make a really sublime, sticky sauce.

1 pound small new potatoes • 4 boneless lamb leg steaks, each about 6 ounces • 2 tablespoons olive oil • 1 teaspoon thyme leaves • 4 tablespoons balsamic vinegar • 2 tablespoons blackberry jam, or to taste • 1 tablespoon butter • 14 ounces broccoli florets • 1 tablespoon chopped parsley leaves • salt and freshly ground black pepper

1 Cook the new potatoes in boiling salted water until tender, 12 to 14 minutes, then drain.
2 Meanwhile, brush the lamb steaks with the olive oil, season with salt and pepper and sprinkle with the thyme. Heat a ridged grill pan over medium-high heat. Grill the lamb until browned, 2 to 3 minutes per side, depending on the thickness of the steaks, or until cooked to your liking.
3 Remove the pan from the heat and stir in the balsamic vinegar, blackberry jam and 2 tablespoons water. Return the pan to low heat and let bubble 1 minute. Add the butter and stir until the sauce is glossy and smooth.
4 While the lamb and sauce are cooking, steam the broccoli until just tender, 4 to 5 minutes.
5 Serve the lamb and blackberry sauce with the broccoli and new potatoes. Scatter the parsley over the potatoes.

STEAK WITH MARSALA MUSTARD CREAM

Marsala, cream and wholegrain mustard make a fabulously tasty quick sauce to accompany tender steak.

4 filet mignons or strip steaks, each about 6 ounces • 4 tablespoons olive oil • 4 tablespoons Marsala • ⅔ cup heavy cream • 1 tablespoon wholegrain mustard, or to taste • 2¼ pounds spinach leaves, washed • juice of ½ lemon • salt and freshly ground black pepper

TO SERVE: sun-dried tomato ciabatta rolls

1 Brush the steaks with half the olive oil and season with salt and pepper. Heat a ridged grill pan or large, nonstick frying pan over high heat. Grill the steaks until cooked to your liking, 2 to 3 minutes per side for rare to medium-rare. Remove from the pan and keep warm.
2 Pour the Marsala into the pan and scrape up any sticky bits with a wooden spoon. Bubble 1 minute over medium heat, then stir in the cream and mustard. Season to taste, then return the steaks briefly to the pan, spooning the sauce over them.
3 Meanwhile, heat the remaining olive oil in a wok or large, nonstick frying pan over high heat. Stir-fry the spinach until wilted, 3 to 4 minutes. Drain off any excess liquid, then squeeze in the lemon juice and season to taste.
4 Serve the steaks with the sauce spooned over, accompanied by the spinach and ciabatta rolls.

TROUT & LENTILS IN WARM CITRUS DRESSING

This dish also works with smoked trout fillets, in which case serve the dressing without heating it.

⅔ cup extra-virgin olive oil • juice of 1 small orange • juice of ½ lemon • 1 teaspoon honey • 1 shallot, chopped • ¼ fennel bulb, trimmed and minced • 8 rainbow trout fillets, each about 4 ounces • 2½ cups pre-cooked vacuum-packed lentils • 1 tablespoon balsamic vinegar • 1 tablespoon chopped parsley leaves • salt and freshly ground black pepper

TO SERVE: green salad

1 Pour two-thirds of the olive oil into a small saucepan. Add the orange and lemon juices and honey. Stir in the shallot and fennel, and season with salt and pepper. Set over low heat to warm gently.
2 Meanwhile, season the trout fillets. Heat 1 tablespoon of the olive oil in a large, nonstick frying pan over medium heat. Cook the trout until just done, about 1 minute per side.
3 While the trout is cooking, put the lentils in a pan with the remaining olive oil and balsamic vinegar. Warm over low heat, stirring occasionally. Stir in the parsley.
4 Serve the trout on the lentils with the dressing drizzled over, and with a salad of green leaves.

SEARED TUNA WITH TOMATO & OLIVE SAUCE

Tuna cooks very quickly; in fact, it should be served pink in the middle. This is the perfect dish for a weekend meal or a dinner party, and without the need to spend hours in the kitchen.

4 tuna steaks, each about 7 ounces • 4 tablespoons olive oil • 1 lemon, thinly sliced • 9 ounces cherry tomatoes • a pinch of sugar • 2 tablespoons salted capers, drained and rinsed • ¾ cup pitted black olives • salt and freshly ground black pepper

TO SERVE: watercress salad and crusty bread

1 Season the tuna with salt and pepper. Heat half the olive oil in a large, nonstick frying pan over high heat. Sear the tuna 1 to 2 minutes on each side, depending on the thickness of the steaks. (Take care not to overcook the fish—it can dry out very quickly.) Remove the tuna from the pan and set aside on a plate, covered to keep warm.
2 Add the lemon slices to the pan and cook until slightly caramelized, 2 to 3 minutes. Stir in the tomatoes, sugar, capers and olives, and cook 5 minutes longer, stirring often.
3 Return the tuna to the pan and heat through 1 minute. Serve the tuna with the sauce spooned over, and with a watercress salad and slices of crusty bread on the side.

CRISP FISH WITH AVOCADO SALSA

Semolina adds a delightful crunch and golden color to white fish fillets—choose cod, haddock or whatever looks good and fresh when you're shopping. A bag of crisp Asian salad greens such as mizuna, baby bok choy and tatsoi would make a great match for the fish and juicy salsa.

4 tablespoons fine semolina or cornmeal • 4 firm white fish fillets, each about 6 ounces • 4 tablespoons extra-virgin olive oil • salt and freshly ground black pepper
AVOCADO SALSA: 1 small red onion, diced • 2 tomatoes, seeded and diced • 2 firm but ripe avocados, pitted and diced • juice of 1 lime • 1 small bunch of cilantro, roughly chopped

TO SERVE: Asian-style salad and ciabatta bread

1 Put the semolina on a plate and season with salt and pepper. Lightly dust both sides of the fish fillets with the semolina to coat.
2 Heat half the olive oil in a large, nonstick frying pan over medium heat. Fry the fish until golden and cooked through, about 2 minutes per side. Drain on paper towels.
3 While the fish is frying, make the salsa. Put the onion, tomatoes and avocados in a bowl. Stir in the remaining olive oil, the lime juice and cilantro, then season to taste. Serve the fish with the avocado salsa, and with a salad of Asian leaves and slices of ciabatta.

< SEARED SALMON, FENNEL & SUGAR SNAP SALAD

Grapefruit is usually considered a breakfast fruit, but here it is the foundation of a delicious sweet-sour dressing. I think you'll be pleasantly surprised by its zingy flavor, which goes particularly well with the salmon salad.

4 skinless salmon fillets, each about 6 ounces • ½ cup extra-virgin olive oil • 2 fennel bulbs, trimmed and thinly sliced • 2 celery stalks, trimmed and thinly sliced diagonally • 4 handfuls of sugar snap peas, cut in half diagonally • juice of 1 pink grapefruit • 1 teaspoon honey, or to taste • salt and freshly ground black pepper

TO SERVE: sourdough bread

1 Season the salmon with salt and pepper. Heat 2 tablespoons of the olive oil in a large, nonstick frying pan over high heat. Sear the salmon until cooked on the outside but still slightly opaque in the center, 3 to 4 minutes on each side, depending on the thickness of the fillets. Cut each fillet into slices.
2 Meanwhile, put the fennel, celery and sugar snap peas in a serving bowl. Whisk the remaining olive oil with the grapefruit juice and honey, then season to taste. Spoon the dressing over the salad and toss.
3 Serve the salad topped with the seared salmon and slices of sourdough bread.

PAN-GRILLED SALMON WITH COCONUT SPINACH

Succulent salmon fillets marry particularly well with creamy, coconut-bathed spinach.

4 salmon fillets, each about 6 ounces • 3 tablespoons olive oil • juice of 1 small lemon • 2 garlic cloves, sliced • 1¾ pounds baby spinach leaves • ½ cup canned coconut cream • ½ teaspoon mild curry paste • salt and freshly ground black pepper

TO SERVE: naan breads

1 Season the salmon fillets with salt and pepper. Heat 2 tablespoons of the olive oil in a ridged grill pan over medium-high heat. Grill the salmon until cooked but still slightly opaque in the center, 3 to 4 minutes on each side, depending on the thickness of the fillets. Squeeze a little lemon juice over each fillet.
2 Meanwhile, heat the remaining oil in a wok or large, nonstick frying pan over medium heat. Stir-fry the garlic 1 minute. Add the spinach and stir-fry until it starts to wilt, 1 to 2 minutes.
3 Mix the coconut cream and curry paste together, then spoon it over the spinach. Stir until combined. Cook until heated through, about 2 minutes, then season to taste. Serve the salmon with the coconut spinach and naan breads on the side.

BAKED EGGS IN SMOKED SALMON CUPS

Eggs and smoked salmon are famously well matched. This makes a tempting, simple dinner.

1 tablespoon softened butter • 4 large slices of smoked salmon • 4 extra-large eggs • 4 heaped tablespoons mascarpone cheese • salt and freshly ground black pepper

TO SERVE: spinach salad and seeded bread

1 Preheat the oven to 400°F.
2 Grease four large ramekins with the butter and line each one with a slice of smoked salmon.
3 Break an egg into each ramekin. Dot the mascarpone evenly across the surface of the eggs and season with salt and pepper. Bake until lightly set, about 10 minutes. Serve with a spinach salad and slices of seeded bread.

FISH IN CHILI BROTH >

Flaky fish in a light, piquant broth, topped with crispy capers... delicious!

4 tablespoons olive oil • 1 onion, chopped • ½ fennel bulb, chopped • 1 teaspoon dried chili flakes • 2½ cups vegetable stock • 14 ounce canned crushed tomatoes, drained • 1 handful of parsley, leaves chopped • 4 skinless white fish fillets, such as cod or haddock, each about 6 ounces • 2 tablespoons salted capers, drained and rinsed • salt and freshly ground black pepper

TO SERVE: crusty bread

1 Heat 2 tablespoons of the olive oil in a large, deep, nonstick frying pan over medium heat. Fry the onion and fennel until softened, about 3 minutes. Stir in the chili flakes.
2 Add the stock, tomatoes and three-fourths of the parsley to the pan and season with salt and pepper. Bring to a boil, then cook over high heat 3 minutes, stirring occasionally.
3 Gently place the fish in the pan. Turn the heat down and simmer until just cooked, 4 to 5 minutes, depending on the thickness of the fillets.
4 Meanwhile, heat the remaining oil in a small, nonstick frying pan and add the capers. Fry over medium heat until golden and crisp, about 2 minutes. Drain on paper towels.
5 Place a fish fillet in each of four shallow soup bowls and spoon the broth over and around. Top with the capers, scatter the remaining parsley over and serve with slices of crusty bread.

< OPEN SARDINE PIADINA

Piadina, which is an Italian-style flatbread, is a specialty of the Emiglia Romana region. Flour tortillas make a good substitute. Ask your fish merchant to prepare the sardines for you.

8 sardines, split open and boned · 3 tablespoons olive oil · juice of 1 lemon · 4 small piadine (or flour tortillas) · 1 red onion, thinly sliced · 12 cherry tomatoes, cut in half · 1 handful of pitted black olives · 1 small handful of parsley, leaves chopped · salt and freshly ground black pepper

TO SERVE: lemon wedges and green salad with herbs

1 Preheat the broiler.
2 Arrange the sardines, skin-side down, in the broiler pan, then drizzle the olive oil and half the lemon juice over them. Broil, 2 to 3 inches from the heat, until cooked, 3 to 4 minutes, then remove and keep warm.
3 Place the piadine under the broiler 1 minute or so to warm through.
4 Scatter half the onion over the warm piadine and add the tomatoes and olives. Lay the sardines on top and squeeze the remaining lemon juice over them. Season with salt and pepper. Finish with a scattering of the remaining onion and parsley. Serve with lemon wedges and a salad of mixed greens and herbs.

SPICED SALMON IN NOODLE MISO BROTH

Use your favorite mild curry powder here—anything too hot will overpower the delicate flavors of the salmon and the miso broth. I sometimes garnish this dish with the crisp fried shallots that you can buy in Asian markets.

3 tablespoons all-purpose flour · 1 tablespoon mild curry powder · 4 salmon fillets, each about 6 ounces · 1 egg white, beaten · 4 tablespoons sunflower oil · 3 tablespoons miso paste · 2 celery stalks, sliced diagonally · 1 bunch of scallions, sliced diagonally · 1 small red chili (mildly hot or hot, to taste), seeded and thinly sliced · 8 ounces dried egg noodles · 1 handful of cilantro, chopped · salt and freshly ground black pepper

1 Mix the flour and curry powder together on a plate. Season with salt and pepper. Brush the salmon fillets lightly with egg white, then turn them in the spiced flour to coat.
2 Heat the sunflower oil in a large, nonstick frying pan over medium heat. Fry the salmon until just cooked, 3 to 4 minutes per side. (The exact timing will depend on the thickness of the fillets, but take care not to overcook them: the fish should still be slightly opaque in the center.)
3 Meanwhile, mix the miso paste with 3¾ cups just-boiled water in a large saucepan. Add the celery, scallions and chili and bring to a boil. Drop in the noodles and stir, then cook until soft, 3 to 4 minutes. Stir in the cilantro. Serve the noodle broth topped with the salmon.

MOROCCAN-SPICED SHRIMP

The spicy marinade for the shrimp is based on a Middle-Eastern paste known as *chermoula*. It also works well with chicken and fish.

1⅔ cups couscous • 500ml/17fl oz/2 cups hot vegetable stock • 2 tablespoons chopped parsley leaves • 3 tablespoons cumin seeds • 1 tablespoon coriander seeds • 1 tablespoon paprika • 1 tablespoon ground ginger • a pinch of dried chili flakes, or to taste • 2 garlic cloves, peeled • 6 tablespoons olive oil • juice of 2 lemons • 1 teaspoon sugar • 2¼ pounds peeled but tail-on, raw jumbo or extra-large shrimp • salt and freshly ground black pepper

TO SERVE: mixed leaf salad

1 Put the couscous in a bowl, and pour the hot stock over to cover. Stir, cover, and let stand until the water is absorbed, 5 to 6 minutes. Fluff up the couscous with a fork and stir in the parsley. Let stand for a few minutes so the flavors can blend.
2 Meanwhile, toast the cumin and coriander seeds in a large, nonstick frying pan until lightly fragrant, about 1 minute. Transfer to a mini blender and add the remaining spices, the garlic and 2 tablespoons of the olive oil. Blend to a paste. Stir in the lemon juice and sugar, then season with salt and pepper.
3 Put the shrimp in a large bowl and spoon the spice paste over. Toss well to coat.
4 Heat the rest of the oil in the frying pan over medium heat. Fry the shrimp until cooked and pink, 3 to 4 minutes. Drain on paper towels. Serve with the couscous and a mixed leaf salad.

THAI SHRIMP & PINEAPPLE CURRY

Juicy shrimp combine well with sweet pineapple, creamy coconut and crunchy green beans in this aromatic curry.

1¼ cups jasmine rice • 2 tablespoons olive oil • 2 garlic cloves, minced • 1 onion, minced • ⅔ cup canned coconut cream • ⅔ cup vegetable stock • 1 tablespoon Thai curry paste • 1 to 2 tablespoons ketchup • 2 handfuls of trimmed green beans • 1 pound cooked, peeled jumbo or extra-large shrimp • 8 ounce canned pineapple chunks in juice, drained • 1 handful of cilantro, chopped • salt and freshly ground black pepper

1 Put the rice in a medium-size saucepan and cover with 2½ cups water. Bring to a boil, then turn the heat down to low, cover and simmer until the rice is cooked and the water absorbed, 10 to 12 minutes.
2 Meanwhile, heat the olive oil in a large saucepan over medium heat. Fry the garlic and onion 2 minutes, then stir in the coconut cream, stock, curry paste and ketchup.
3 Add the green beans and cook 2 minutes. Add the shrimp and pineapple, and season with salt and pepper. Cook until the sauce has reduced and thickened, about 3 minutes. Stir in the cilantro and serve with the jasmine rice.

CREOLE SHRIMP

These crisp, coconut-coated shrimp make a lively combo with the spicy Creole sauce.

1⅓ cups giant couscous • 1 teaspoon cumin seeds • ½ cup sunflower oil • 1 small onion, minced • 1 garlic clove, minced • 14 ounces canned crushed tomatoes • 2 tablespoons dark brown sugar • 1 teaspoon dried oregano • ½ teaspoon hot chili powder • 2¼ pounds peeled (but tail-on) raw jumbo or extra-large shrimp • 1 egg white, beaten • 1½ cups dried shredded coconut • salt and freshly ground black pepper

TO SERVE: green salad

1 Cook the couscous in a saucepan of boiling salted water until tender, 6 to 8 minutes; drain and set aside, covered, until ready to serve.
2 Meanwhile, toast the cumin seeds in a nonstick frying pan until lightly fragrant, about 30 seconds.
3 Pour in 2 tablespoons of the sunflower oil, then add the onion and garlic and fry over medium-high heat 30 seconds. Add the tomatoes, sugar, oregano, chili powder, and salt and pepper to taste.
4 Bring to a boil, then turn the heat down to medium-low and simmer until reduced and thickened, about 10 minutes.
5 While the Creole sauce is cooking, dip the shrimp in the egg white and then in the coconut to coat.
6 Heat the remaining oil in a large, deep frying pan and fry the shrimp, turning once, until golden and cooked through, 3 to 4 minutes. Drain on paper towels and sprinkle with a little salt.
7 Serve the shrimp with the Creole sauce, giant couscous and a crisp green salad.

WARM CARAMELIZED APPLE & GOAT CHEESE SALAD

There are few more agreeable combinations than a juicy apple paired with tasty cheese, especially when the apples are caramelized in butter and honey, and the cheese is a tangy goat cheese!

¼ stick butter • 2 crisp apples, cored and sliced • 2 tablespoons honey • 3 tablespoons apple cider vinegar • 4 tablespoons extra-virgin olive oil • 4 handfuls of arugula • 1 pound goat cheese log (or similar), crumbled • 1 small handful of walnut halves • salt and freshly ground black pepper

TO SERVE: rye bread

1 Melt the butter in a frying pan over medium heat. Sauté the apples with a pinch of salt until softened, 3 to 4 minutes. Add the honey and bubble until the apples caramelize, about 1 minute. Remove from the heat and stir in the cider vinegar and olive oil.
2 Lightly toss together the arugula leaves, goat cheese and walnuts. Add the apples, spooning any pan juices over, then season with pepper. Serve with rye bread.

THREE-CHEESE PHYLLO TARTS

These light, crisp and golden tarts are really simple and speedy to make. If you want to experiment, try your own favorite combination of cheeses and replace the sun-dried tomatoes with jarred artichokes or mushrooms in oil, drained.

8 (6-inch) squares of phyllo pastry • ½ stick butter, melted • 1 heaped cup grated Gruyère cheese • ¾ cup grated Parmesan cheese • ½ cup mascarpone • 12 sun-dried tomatoes in oil, drained and chopped • 8 basil leaves • salt and freshly ground black pepper

TO SERVE: fruity chutney, green salad with herbs and crusty bread

1 Preheat the oven to 400°F.
2 Take two squares of pastry and lay them on top of each other at an angle to form a star shape. Brush lightly with melted butter and place buttered-side down in one cup of a muffin top pan. Repeat to make three more tart shells. Brush with a little extra butter and bake until light golden and crisp, 3 to 4 minutes.
3 Meanwhile, mix the three cheeses together in a large bowl and stir in the sun-dried tomatoes and basil. Season with salt and pepper. Divide the mixture among the cooked tart shells and return them to the oven to bake until the cheese is melted and golden, 3 to 4 minutes.
4 Serve the tarts hot with a spoonful of chutney, a salad of mixed greens and herbs, and slices of crusty bread.

BOX-BAKED CAMEMBERT

This is just like a cheese fondue in a box, only much easier to make and fabulous for sharing. Alternatively, you can scoop the cheese out onto plates and serve with an arugula salad.

2 whole, wooden-boxed Camembert cheeses • 4 garlic cloves, cut into thin slices • 16 small, young thyme sprigs • 6 tablespoons dry white wine • 4 tablespoons extra-virgin olive oil • freshly ground black pepper

TO SERVE: sourdough or country-style bread and vegetable crudités

1 Preheat the oven to 400°F.
2 Take each Camembert out of its box and remove the inner wrapper. Using the point of a sharp knife, make random shallow cuts into each cheese. Insert a slice of garlic and sprig of thyme into each slit. Return the cheeses to their wooden boxes.
3 Spoon the wine over the surface and add a grinding of black pepper. Place the boxes on a baking sheet and bake until the cheese is soft and melted inside, 6 to 8 minutes. Serve with slices of bread and vegetable crudités.

"POOR MAN'S PARMESAN" PASTA

In Italy, crisply fried bread crumbs were traditionally used as a cheap substitute for Parmesan by those who couldn't afford the real thing. I think they make a wonderful alternative.

1 pound dried penne pasta • 4 tablespoons extra-virgin olive oil • 1¼ cups fine white bread crumbs • 1 heaped cup mascarpone cheese • grated zest of 2 lemons • salt and freshly ground black pepper

TO SERVE: mixed leaf salad

1 Bring a large pan of salted water to a boil and cook the penne until al dente, about 10 minutes.
2 Meanwhile, heat the olive oil in a large, nonstick frying pan over medium heat. Fry the bread crumbs until golden, 2 to 3 minutes. Remove from the heat and season with a little salt. Set aside.
3 Mix the mascarpone and lemon zest together and season with a little pepper. Drain the cooked pasta and toss with the lemon mascarpone. Scatter the golden crumbs over the pasta, then serve with a mixed leaf salad.

FRESH MINT & PEA PESTO CAVATAPPI >

Cavatappi are whirly spirals of pasta that catch the lovely, vibrant homemade pesto here, but any pasta shape would do.

1 pound dried cavatappi pasta • salt and freshly ground black pepper
PEA & MINT PESTO: 2 cups frozen peas • 4 tablespoons extra-virgin olive oil • 2 garlic cloves, minced • ⅔ cup blanched almonds, chopped • 1 cup grated Parmesan cheese, plus extra for serving • 5 to 6 mint leaves • a pinch of sugar

TO SERVE: green salad

1 Bring a large saucepan of salted water to a boil and cook the cavatappi until al dente, about 10 minutes.
2 Meanwhile, cook the peas in boiling water until just tender, 2 to 3 minutes. Drain and transfer to a blender. Add the olive oil, garlic and almonds, then blitz to a coarse paste. Add the Parmesan and mint and blitz again, then season with a little sugar, salt and pepper.
3 Drain the pasta and toss with the pesto. Sprinkle with extra Parmesan, if desired, and serve with a salad of mixed greens.

BIG-BOWL MINESTRONE

Frozen bags of mixed veggies are a great standby to have on hand—they're a boon if you're short of time and healthy, too.

2 tablespoons olive oil • 1 onion, chopped • 1 pound mixed frozen vegetables • 2½ cups vegetable stock • 14 ounces canned crushed tomatoes • 1⅓ cups small dried pasta, such as ditaline, farfalline or vermicelli • 14 ounces canned cannellini beans, drained and rinsed • 1 small handful of parsley, leaves chopped • salt and freshly ground black pepper

TO SERVE: country-style bread

1 Heat the olive oil in a large saucepan over medium heat. Fry the onion until softened, about 2 minutes. Add the vegetables and stock and bring to a boil. Stir in the tomatoes, season with salt and pepper, and cook 2 to 3 minutes.
2 Add the pasta and beans, return to almost boiling point and cook, stirring occasionally, until the pasta is al dente and the soup has thickened, about 8 minutes. Stir in the parsley and serve with slices of country-style bread.

SPICY COCONUT & CHICKPEA SOUP

This filling and soothing soup makes a great dinner on a cold winter's night.

2 tablespoons olive oil • 2 garlic cloves, minced • 1 onion, chopped • 1 celery stalk, minced • ⅔ cup canned coconut cream • 2½ cups vegetable stock • 14 ounces canned chickpeas, drained • 2 large handfuls of baby spinach leaves • 1 long red chili (mildly hot or hot, to taste), seeded and shredded

1 Heat the olive oil in a large saucepan over medium heat. Fry the garlic, onion and celery until softened, about 3 minutes.
2 Add the coconut cream and stock and stir well to mix. Bring to a boil, then turn the heat down and simmer 2 minutes.
3 Add the chickpeas and simmer until the soup is slightly reduced and thickened, about 5 minutes. Stir in the spinach and chili, then cook until the spinach has wilted, about 2 minutes. Serve hot.

MISO & TOFU SOUP WITH WONTONS

Crisp-fried wonton skins make an unusual garnish for this easy soup. You may need to adjust the quantity of miso, according to the brand you are using, since some are more concentrated than others. Note that the lighter the color, the milder the flavor.

3 to 4 heaped teaspoons brown miso paste • 1 small bunch of scallions, chopped • 2-inch piece fresh ginger root, peeled and sliced • 7 ounces cremini mushrooms, sliced • 1 head of napa cabbage, shredded • 1 pound firm tofu, patted dry and cubed • 6 tablespoons sunflower oil • 4 wonton skins, cut into thin strips

1 Pour 3¾ cups hot water into a large saucepan and stir in the miso paste. Add the scallions, ginger and mushrooms, then bring the soup back to a boil.
2 Add the napa cabbage and tofu, turn the heat down and simmer until the leaves have wilted and the tofu is heated through, about 3 minutes.
3 Meanwhile, heat the sunflower oil in a wok or frying pan until very hot. Fry the wonton strips until golden and crisp, about 2 minutes. Drain on paper towels. Serve the soup topped with the crispy wonton ribbons.

NOW THAT YOU'VE SEEN — AND HOPEFULLY TASTED — IN EARLIER CHAPTERS WHAT AMAZING DISHES CAN BE ACHIEVED IN A VERY SHORT AMOUNT OF TIME, TWENTY MINUTES IS GOING TO SEEM POSITIVELY LUXURIOUS! HERE, I'VE INCLUDED A MIXED SHELLFISH COLOMBO FROM THE CARIBBEAN, THAI-SIZZLED LAMB AND A SIMPLE SWISS CHEESE FONDUE.

TWENTY-MINUTE MEALS

GRILLED GREMOLATA-CRUSTED CHICKEN

Gremolata is the classic Italian garnish for *osso bucco* (slow-cooked veal), but it seems a shame not to eat it with other types of dishes, too.

1 pound baby new potatoes • 1 tablespoon butter • 4 skinless, boneless chicken breast halves, each about 6 ounces • 2 garlic cloves, minced • 1 handful of parsley, leaves chopped • grated zest of 2 lemons • 2 tablespoons olive oil • salt and freshly ground black pepper

TO SERVE: mixed leaf salad

1 Cook the potatoes in a pan of boiling salted water until tender, about 15 minutes. Drain and toss with the butter.
2 While the potatoes are cooking, use a rolling pin or meat mallet to flatten the chicken breasts slightly.
3 Mix the garlic, parsley and three-fourths of the lemon zest together in a bowl, and season with salt and pepper. Scatter the mixture over the chicken and press it into the meat until evenly coated.
4 Heat the oil in a ridged grill pan. Grill the chicken over medium-high heat until cooked, about 3 to 4 minutes per side. Scatter the remaining lemon zest over and serve with the potatoes and a salad.

TWICE-COOKED CRISP CHICKEN WITH SESAME CABBAGE

I love this combination of sticky, sweet, salty and spicy flavors that coat the chicken breasts. If I'm in a real hurry, I sometimes cheat and just buy a freshly roasted chicken.

2½ cups chicken stock • 4 skinless, boneless chicken breast halves, each about 6 ounces • 2 tablespoons all-purpose flour • 2 teaspoons dark brown sugar • 2 teaspoons ground ginger • 4 tablespoons sunflower oil • 1 head of Savoy cabbage, leaves shredded • ¼ cup sesame seeds • 9 ounces dried egg noodles • 2 tablespoons toasted sesame oil • salt and freshly ground black pepper

1 Bring the stock to a boil in a large saucepan. Add the chicken breasts and poach 5 minutes.
2 Meanwhile, mix together the flour, sugar and ginger in a bowl, and season with salt and pepper. Using a slotted spoon, remove the chicken from the pan and shred using two forks. Dredge in the flour.
3 Heat half the oil in a wok or large, nonstick frying pan. Fry the chicken, turning halfway, until dark and slightly crisp, 3 to 4 minutes. Drain on paper towels and keep warm.
4 Heat the rest of the oil in the cleaned wok or frying pan. Stir-fry the cabbage with the sesame seeds until just tender, 3 to 4 minutes; season to taste.
5 At the same time, bring a pan of salted water to a boil and cook the noodles until soft, 3 to 4 minutes. Drain and toss with the sesame oil. Serve the chicken with the cabbage and noodles.

CHICKEN CUTLETS IN RICH TOMATO SAUCE

The combination of golden chicken and basil-infused tomato sauce is really popular in my house and I hope it will be in yours, too.

¼ cup all-purpose flour • 4 thin chicken cutlets, each about 6 ounces • 4 tablespoons olive oil • salt and freshly ground black pepper
TOMATO SAUCE: 3 tablespoons olive oil • 1 onion, minced • 2 garlic cloves, minced • 14 ounces canned crushed tomatoes • 2 teaspoons sugar • 1 small handful of basil leaves, roughly torn

TO SERVE: watercress salad and crusty bread

1 To make the tomato sauce, heat the olive oil in a saucepan over medium heat. Fry the onion and garlic until softened, about 2 minutes.
2 Add the tomatoes and sugar, and season with salt and pepper. Bring to a boil, then turn the heat down and simmer until glossy and thickened, 10 to 15 minutes. Stir in the basil.
3 Meanwhile, spread the flour on a plate and season with salt and pepper. Coat the chicken cutlets in the seasoned flour and shake to remove any excess.
4 Heat the olive oil in a large, nonstick frying pan. Fry the chicken until golden and cooked through, about 4 minutes per side. Serve with the tomato sauce alongside, a watercress salad and slices of crusty bread.

BALINESE SPICY CHICKEN SOUP

This fragrant soup is based on a dish I ate in Bali. The Balinese tend to use aromatic spice pastes as the foundation of a dish, but the exact quantities of flavorings aren't set in stone. So feel free to experiment according to how mild or fiery-hot you like your food.

2 shallots, chopped • 1 lemongrass stalk, minced • 1-inch piece fresh ginger root, peeled and roughly chopped • 1 garlic clove, minced • 1 tablespoon palm sugar or brown sugar • 2 small red chilies (mildly hot or hot, to taste) • 1 small handful of cashew nuts or macadamia nuts • 2 tablespoons sunflower oil • 1 pound ground chicken • 4 cups chicken stock • 3 kaffir lime leaves, shredded

1 Put the shallots, lemongrass, ginger, garlic, palm sugar and 1 chili in a food processor and blitz to a paste. Add the cashew nuts and blitz again to make a coarse paste.
2 Heat the sunflower oil in a large saucepan over high heat. Fry the paste 30 seconds, stirring constantly.
3 Add the chicken and fry until it is beginning to color, 2 to 3 minutes. Pour in the stock and bring to a boil, then turn the heat down and simmer until the chicken is cooked, about 12 minutes.
4 Meanwhile, finely slice the remaining chili. Stir the lime leaves into the soup and scatter the sliced chili over the top before serving.

SAUSAGE & RED WINE FUSILLI

Cook the pasta for a little less time than suggested on the package, then finish cooking it in the sauce so the gutsy flavors infuse the fusilli.

2 tablespoons olive oil • 2 garlic cloves, sliced • 6 fresh pork link sausages (Italian, if possible), split open• 1¼ cups red wine • ½ teaspoon sugar • 4 thyme sprigs • 1 pound dried fusilli pasta • salt and freshly ground black pepper • grated Parmesan cheese for serving

TO SERVE: green salad

1 Heat the oil in a large, deep, nonstick sauté pan over medium heat. Add the garlic and crumble the sausage into the pan,discarding the skins. Fry, turning often, until browned, about 5 minutes.
2 Pour in the wine and add the sugar and thyme. Bring to a boil, then turn the heat down and simmer until the wine has reduced, about 10 minutes. Season with salt and pepper.
3 Meanwhile, bring a large saucepan of salted water to a boil. Cook the fusilli until almost al dente (about 2 minutes less than directed on the package).
4 Remove the pasta from the pan using a slotted spoon and transfer to the sauté pan. Stir, then cook until the pasta is al dente, about 2 minutes. Sprinkle the pasta with grated Parmesan and serve with a salad of mixed greens.

CRISP HAM SALAD WITH HONEY & MUSTARD DRESSING

This is a great way to use up cooked ham, but it's also worth buying ham specially for the salad. You'll need very thick slices.

¼ cup all-purpose flour • 1 pound cooked ham in thick slices, shredded • sunflower oil, for frying • 8 slices of ciabatta bread • 4 large handfuls of mixed salad greens • 1 handful of cherry tomatoes, cut in half • ½ hothouse cucumber, sliced • 4 scallions, sliced • 1 carrot, cut into ribbons
HONEY & MUSTARD DRESSING: 1 cup heavy cream • 1 tablespoon wholegrain mustard • 1 tablespoon honey • salt and freshly ground black pepper

1 Put the flour in a plastic bag and season with salt and pepper. Add the ham and shake to coat.
2 Heat the sunflower oil in a large, nonstick frying pan over high heat. Fry the ham until crisp and golden, 3 to 4 minutes. Drain on paper towels.
3 Meanwhile, make the dressing. Mix together the cream, mustard and honey. Loosen with a little water, if necessary, then season to taste.
4 Heat a ridged grill pan until hot. Grill the slices of ciabatta to toast and char, about 2 minutes per side.
5 Place the salad greens on serving plates and top with the tomato, cucumber, scallions, carrot and crisp ham. Drizzle the dressing over and serve with the grilled ciabatta on the side.

CHEESE & PROSCIUTTO CROSTATA

It's important to have the oven preheated so the pastry cooks quickly. If you can only find frozen puff pastry, be sure to let it thaw before use.

1 sheet of chilled puff pastry, about 13 ounces
• 2 eggs, beaten • 1 cup grated Parmesan cheese
• 4 ounces prosciutto, torn into pieces • ½ heaped cup taleggio cheese, cut into cubes

TO SERVE: tomato and arugula salad

1 Preheat the oven to 425°F.
2 Lay the pastry on a large baking sheet and turn over the edges to form a ½-inch raised border.
3 Beat the eggs and Parmesan together and spoon over the pastry, spreading it out evenly, up to the border. Scatter the prosciutto and taleggio on top. Bake until the pastry is golden, 10 to 12 minutes. Serve with a tomato and arugula salad.

SWEET SOY & PINEAPPLE PORK

Pork tenderloin is succulent and easy-to-use. Here it's teamed with juicy chunks of pineapple and a delectable dark, sticky sauce.

1¼ cups long-grain rice • 2 tablespoons dark soy sauce • 2 tablespoons honey • 2 tablespoons Shaoxing wine or dry sherry • ⅔ cup vegetable or meat stock • 2 teaspoons cornstarch • 2 tablespoons sunflower oil • 1 pound pork tenderloin, sliced • 2 garlic cloves, sliced • 1 cup unsalted cashew nuts • 1 cup fresh pineapple cubes

1 Put the rice in a medium-size saucepan and cover with 2½ cups water. Bring to a boil, then turn the heat down, cover and simmer until the rice is cooked and the water absorbed, 15 minutes. Remove from the heat and let stand, covered, until ready to serve.
2 While the rice is cooking, mix the soy sauce, honey, Shaoxing wine and stock together. Stir in the cornstarch. Set aside.
3 Heat the sunflower oil in a wok or large, nonstick frying pan over high heat. Stir-fry the pork with the garlic until golden, 5 to 6 minutes.
4 Add the cashew nuts and stir-fry until they are light golden, about 2 minutes. Stir in the pineapple and cook until heated through, 3 to 4 minutes.
5 Turn the heat down a little and pour in the soy sauce mixture. Cook, stirring, until the sauce has thickened, about 2 minutes. Serve the pork stir-fry with the rice.

SOUVLAKI WITH CILANTRO & GARLIC YOGURT DIP

These lamb skewers are served with a classic Greek garlicky yogurt dip. You will need 8 metal skewers that fit into your grill pan.

1 pound lean ground lamb • 1 onion, minced • 1 garlic clove, minced • 3 tablespoons Worcestershire sauce • 2 tablespoons olive oil • salt and freshly ground black pepper
CILANTRO & GARLIC YOGURT DIP: 2½ cups thick, whole-milk plain yogurt • 2 garlic cloves, minced • 1 handful of cilantro, chopped

TO SERVE: pita breads and green salad

1 Mix the lamb with the onion, garlic and Worcestershire sauce, and season with salt and pepper. Divide the mixture into eight, then form each portion into a long sausage shape around a skewer.
2 Heat a ridged grill pan over medium-high heat. Brush the lamb with the olive oil and grill until well browned and cooked, 3 to 4 minutes per side. (You may need to cook the skewers in two batches.)
3 Meanwhile, to make the cilantro and garlic yogurt dip, mix all the ingredients together in a bowl and season to taste. Serve the souvlaki with the dip, pita breads and a salad of mixed greens.

THAI-SIZZLED LAMB

Lamb goes really well with Thai flavors and responds perfectly to being cooked quickly.

1¼ cups jasmine rice • 2 tablespoons sunflower oil • 1 lemongrass stalk, peeled and minced • 2 garlic cloves, sliced • 1 pound boneless lamb from the leg, thinly sliced • 2 bell peppers (1 red and 1 yellow), seeded and thinly sliced • 3 tablespoons fish sauce • 3 tablespoons palm sugar or brown sugar • 1 handful of cherry tomatoes, cut into quarters • ½ hothouse cucumber, peeled, seeded and diced • 6 scallions, sliced • 2 tablespoons chopped salted peanuts • 1 handful of mint, chopped

1 Put the rice in a medium-size saucepan and cover with 2½ cups water. Bring to a boil, then turn the heat down to low, cover and simmer until the rice is cooked and the water absorbed, 10 to 12 minutes.
2 Meanwhile, heat the oil in a wok or large, nonstick frying pan over high heat. Stir-fry the lemongrass and garlic 1 minute. Add the lamb and peppers and stir-fry 2 to 3 minutes.
3 Mix the fish sauce and palm sugar together. Add to the wok and stir-fry 2 minutes, then add the tomatoes and cucumber and toss again. Stir in the scallions, peanuts and mint and serve with the jasmine rice.

GLAZED LAMB CHOPS WITH GARLIC SAUCE

Easy and sublime...

1 pound baby new potatoes • 2 tablespoons red-currant jelly • 2 tablespoons Worcestershire sauce • 8 to 12 lamb chops, depending on size **GARLIC SAUCE:** 2 cups heavy cream • 8 garlic cloves, peeled • 4 thyme sprigs • 2 salted anchovies in oil, drained • 1 tablespoon wholegrain mustard • 1 small handful of parsley, leaves chopped • 2¼ pounds baby spinach leaves, washed • salt and freshly ground black pepper

1 Preheat the broiler.
2 Cook the new potatoes in a saucepan of boiling salted water until tender, about 15 minutes; drain.
3 Meanwhile, make the sauce. Put the cream in a pan with the garlic and thyme. Bring to a boil, then turn the heat down and simmer until the sauce has reduced and thickened, about 10 minutes. Add the anchovies and stir for a few minutes until they disintegrate into the sauce. Stir in the mustard and parsley, then season with salt and pepper.
4 While the sauce is simmering, mix the red-currant jelly and Worcestershire sauce together and brush over the chops. Broil, brushing with the jelly mixture halfway through, until well browned and glazed, 4 to 5 minutes per side. Remove from the heat and season to taste.
5 At the same time, cook the spinach in a pan, with only the water left clinging to the leaves after washing, until wilted, 2 to 3 minutes. Season to taste. Serve the lamb with the garlic sauce, spinach and new potatoes.

SLOPPY JOES

"Sloppy" refers to the way that the savory filling oozes out of the bun as you eat it. Be sure to have plenty of paper napkins on hand.

2 tablespoons olive oil • 1 garlic clove, minced • 1 onion, chopped • 1 pound lean ground beef • 14 ounces canned crushed tomatoes • 1 teaspoon sugar • 2 tablespoons Worcestershire sauce • 2 tablespoons dark soy sauce • 1 dried bay leaf • salt and freshly ground black pepper

TO SERVE: 4 hamburger buns, split in half, and mixed leaf salad

1 Heat the olive oil in a large saucepan over medium-high heat. Fry the garlic and onion 1 minute. Add the beef and cook, stirring frequently, until browned, 3 to 4 minutes.
2 Stir in the tomatoes, sugar, Worcestershire sauce, soy sauce and bay leaf, and season with salt and pepper. Bring to a boil, then turn the heat down and simmer over medium heat until reduced and thickened, about 10 minutes. Remove and discard the bay leaf.
3 Just before you are ready to serve, toast the buns. Place one half on each serving plate and spoon the beef mixture on top. Add the other half of each bun. Serve with a mixed leaf salad.

GINGER BEEF & CASHEW NOODLES >

Cucumber is surprisingly delicious hot, and its subtle flavor works well with beef in this robust sauce. Look for palm sugar in health-food stores and Asian markets.

8 ounces dried egg noodles • 1 tablespoon toasted sesame oil • 1 small hothouse cucumber, peeled, seeded and diced • 2 tablespoons soy sauce • 1 tablespoon fish sauce • 1 tablespoon palm sugar or brown sugar • 1 tablespoon rice wine vinegar • 2 tablespoons sunflower oil • 8 minute steaks, cut into strips • 2 garlic cloves, chopped • 2-inch piece candied ginger, chopped • 1 small bunch of scallions, chopped • 2 celery stalks, sliced • 2 handfuls of unsalted cashew nuts • 2 tablespoons chopped cilantro leaves • salt

1 Bring a pan of salted water to a boil and cook the noodles until soft, 3 to 4 minutes. Drain and rinse under cold running water. Toss the noodles in the sesame oil and set aside.
2 While the noodles are cooking, toss the diced cucumber in salt and place in a colander. Let drain 3 minutes, then rinse and drain again.
3 Mix the soy sauce, fish sauce, palm sugar and rice wine vinegar together.
4 Heat the sunflower oil in a wok or large, nonstick frying pan over high heat. Stir-fry the steak with the garlic and ginger until the steak is browned, about 2 minutes. Add the scallions, celery and cashew nuts and stir-fry 2 minutes longer.
5 Add the cucumber and stir-fry 2 minutes. Toss in the noodles and the soy sauce mixture and heat through 1 to 2 minutes, turning to mix. Scatter the cilantro over and serve.

SEARED STEAKS WITH ROMESCO-STYLE SAUCE

The inspiration for this recipe is Spanish romesco sauce, which is traditionally made with special romesco peppers and thickened with bread and nuts. Here, chili oil is used in place of the peppers.

3 tablespoons extra-virgin olive oil, plus extra for brushing • 2 large slices of country-style bread, crusts removed and torn into bite-size pieces • 2 garlic cloves, minced • ⅓ cup whole hazelnuts • 6 plum (roma) tomatoes, seeded and roughly chopped • 2 to 3 tablespoons sherry vinegar • 2 to 3 tablespoons chili oil, or to taste • 2 teaspoons sugar • 4 boneless sirloin steaks, each about 6 ounces • salt and freshly ground black pepper

TO SERVE: country-style bread and green salad

1 To make the romesco-style sauce, heat 2 tablespoons of the olive oil in a large, nonstick frying pan over medium heat. Fry the bread, garlic and hazelnuts, stirring occasionally, until everything takes on a golden color, 2 to 3 minutes. Transfer to a food processor.
2 Heat the remaining olive oil in the frying pan. Fry the tomatoes until they just start to soften, about 3 minutes. Transfer to the food processor and blitz with the bread mixture to a coarse paste. Add the sherry vinegar, chili oil and sugar, then blitz briefly again. Season with salt and pepper to taste.
3 Heat a ridged grill pan until very hot. Brush the steaks with oil and season, then sear until cooked to your liking, about 3 minutes per side for rare steaks. Serve with the sauce, slices of bread and a green salad.

SALADE NIÇOISE

This classic salad, which combines the flavors typical of Nice and the French Riviera, makes a great summer dish.

12 ounces baby new potatoes • 4 eggs • 4 handfuls of trimmed green beans • 1 small handful of salted capers, drained and rinsed • 1 handful of pitted black olives • 2 cups sliced jarred, roasted red bell peppers in olive oil, drained • 6 salted anchovy fillets, rinsed and patted dry • 1 pound jarred or canned tuna in olive oil, flaked into chunks • 4 handfuls of mixed salad greens
DRESSING: 7 tablespoons extra-virgin olive oil • 2 tablespoons white wine vinegar • 1 teaspoon Dijon mustard • 1 to 2 teaspoons sugar • salt and freshly ground black pepper

TO SERVE: crusty bread

1 Cook the potatoes in boiling salted water until tender, 12 to 15 minutes. Drain and transfer to a large bowl.
2 Meanwhile, hard-cook the eggs for 5 minutes. Rinse under cold running water, then peel the eggs and cut into quarters; set aside.
3 At the same time, blanch the green beans in boiling water 2 minutes; drain and rinse under cold running water. Add the green beans, capers, olives, roasted red peppers, anchovies and tuna to the bowl with the potatoes.
4 Put all the ingredients for the dressing in a tightly capped jar and shake until emulsified. Season the dressing with salt and pepper, then pour it over the potato and tuna mixture. Toss gently until everything is combined and coated in dressing.
5 Arrange the salad leaves on a platter and spoon the potato and tuna mixture over. Arrange the eggs on top and serve with crusty bread.

SESAME-CRUSTED SALMON WITH DIP >

Sesame seeds have a delightfully delicate crunchy texture and a nutty flavor that goes superbly well with salmon.

finely grated zest of 1 lime • 6 tablespoons sesame seeds • 4 salmon fillets, each about 6 ounces • 1 egg white, beaten • 3 tablespoons sunflower oil • 9 ounces dried egg noodles • 1 tablespoon toasted sesame oil • 2 tablespoons soy sauce • salt and freshly ground black pepper
DIPPING SAUCE: 2 scallions, chopped • ½ cup Japanese plum vinegar • 2 tablespoons Worcestershire sauce • 1 tablespoon chopped cilantro, plus extra for garnish

TO SERVE: lime wedges and spinach salad

1 Mix the lime zest and sesame seeds together on a plate and season with salt and pepper. Brush the salmon fillets lightly with egg white, then coat them in the sesame seed mixture.
2 Heat the sunflower oil in a large, nonstick frying pan over medium heat. Fry the salmon until the sesame seeds are golden and the fish is cooked but still slightly opaque in the center, 3 to 4 minutes on each side.
3 Meanwhile, bring a pan of salted water to a boil and cook the noodles until soft, 3 to 4 minutes. Drain and toss with the sesame oil and soy sauce.
4 To make the dipping sauce, mix half of the scallions with the rest of the ingredients. Place a salmon fillet on each serving plate with a portion of noodles. Sprinkle with the remaining scallions and some cilantro. Serve with lime wedges and a spinach salad.

LOBSTER & HERB SALAD WITH LEMON MAYO

This is a beautiful dish and makes a luxurious summery meal.

1 ¾ pounds freshly cooked lobster meat, cut into bite-size pieces • 1 large avocado, pitted and diced • 4 ripe but firm tomatoes, seeded and diced • 4 handfuls of mixed salad greens and herb leaves • salt and freshly ground black pepper
LEMON MAYONNAISE: 1 egg • juice of ½ lemon, plus extra to taste • 1 teaspoon Dijon mustard • 1 ¼ cups sunflower oil

TO SERVE: olive bread

1 To make the mayonnaise, put the egg, lemon juice, mustard and a pinch of salt in a blender. Switch the motor on and slowly trickle in the sunflower oil until the mixture starts to emulsify and thicken; continue adding the oil a bit more quickly until it has all been incorporated. Taste and add more salt and lemon juice, if needed.
2 Put the lobster meat and avocado in a bowl. Add the tomatoes and season to taste. Gently stir in enough mayonnaise to coat lightly.
3 Arrange the salad and herb leaves on a serving plate and top with the lobster salad. Serve with slices of olive bread.

SEA BASS WITH CREAMY DILL SAUCE

The creamy sauce here is given an extra kick with chopped capers. It is a perfect partner for broiled sea bass fillets.

1 pound baby new potatoes • 1¼ cups heavy cream • 1 garlic clove, cut in half • grated zest and juice of 1 lemon • 2 tablespoons salted capers, rinsed, drained and chopped • 1 tablespoon chopped dill • 4 large sea bass fillets • 5 tablespoons olive oil • 3 cups frozen petite peas • salt and freshly ground black pepper

1 Cook the potatoes in boiling salted water until tender, 12 to 15 minutes; drain. Preheat the broiler.
2 Meanwhile, pour the cream into a saucepan and add the garlic. Place the pan over low heat and add the lemon zest, capers and dill. Season with salt and pepper. Simmer gently until slightly thickened, 3 to 4 minutes; keep warm.
3 Arrange the sea bass fillets in a heatproof dish and drizzle 2 tablespoons of the olive oil over them. Squeeze a little lemon juice over each fillet and season to taste. Broil the fish, 3 to 4 inches from the heat, until just cooked through, about 6 minutes.
4 At the same time, cook the peas in boiling salted water 3 to 4 minutes; drain.
5 Heat the remaining oil in a large, nonstick frying pan over medium heat. Fry the potatoes until golden, 3 to 4 minutes. Serve the sea bass with the dill sauce, peas and sautéed potatoes.

CRISP FISH GOUJONS

Golden, cornmeal-coated goujons are served with a delicious caper and chive mayonnaise. Mayonnaise is remarkably quick and easy to make, and tastes much better than any you buy.

6 tablespoons fine cornmeal • 4 skinless white fish fillets, each about 6 ounces, cut into ⅝-inch strips • ½ cup milk • 4 tablespoons sunflower oil • 3 cups frozen petite peas • salt and freshly ground black pepper
CAPER MAYONNAISE: 1 egg • juice of ½ lemon • 1 teaspoon Dijon mustard • 1¼ cups sunflower oil • 1 tablespoon capers, drained, rinsed and chopped • 1 tablespoon chopped chives

TO SERVE: crusty bread

1 To make the caper mayonnaise, put the egg, lemon juice, mustard and a pinch of salt in a blender. Switch the motor on and slowly trickle in the sunflower oil until the mixture starts to emulsify and thicken; continue adding the oil more quickly until it has all been incorporated. Pour the mayonnaise into a bowl and stir in the capers and chives.
2 Spread the cornmeal on a plate and season with salt and pepper. Dip the fish goujons into the milk and press into the cornmeal to coat.
3 Heat the sunflower oil in a large, nonstick frying pan over medium-high heat. Fry the fish until golden and crisp, 2 to 3 minutes. (You may have to do this in two batches.) Remove from the pan and drain on paper towels.
4 While you are frying the fish, cook the peas in boiling salted water 3 to 4 minutes; drain. Serve the goujons hot with the caper mayonnaise, peas and slices of crusty bread.

TOMATO & CHILI MUSSELS

Mussels are very versatile—they're delicious in creamy sauces, and also work really well with tomatoes and chili. The juice from the drained tomatoes is not used in this recipe, but can be kept for use in another dish.

2 tablespoons olive oil • 2 garlic cloves, sliced • 2¼ pounds mussels, cleaned • ½ cup dry white wine • 28 ounces canned crushed tomatoes, drained • 1 teaspoon dried chili flakes

TO SERVE: crusty bread and green salad

1 Heat the olive oil in a large saucepan over medium heat. Fry the garlic 30 seconds, then add the mussels and white wine.
2 Add the tomatoes and chili flakes to the pan and stir well. Bring to a boil, then turn the heat down slightly, cover and cook until all the shells have opened, about 5 minutes.
3 Serve in large bowls, with crusty bread to mop up the juices and a green salad.

MIXED SHELLFISH COLOMBO >

A *Colombo* is a type of curry indigenous to the French Caribbean islands. If you can't find Colombo spice powder, simply substitute a mild curry powder of your choice.

1¼ cups long-grain rice • 2 tablespoons olive oil • 1 onion, chopped • 2 garlic cloves, chopped • 1-inch piece fresh ginger root, peeled and chopped • 1 tablespoon Colombo powder (or mild curry powder) • 1¼ cups canned coconut milk • ⅔ cup vegetable stock • 2 pounds raw mixed shellfish, cleaned and prepared as necessary • juice of 2 limes • 1 to 2 tablespoons mango chutney • 2 tablespoons ketchup • 1 handful of parsley, leaves chopped • salt and freshly ground black pepper

1 Put the rice in a medium-sized saucepan and cover with 2½ cups water. Bring to a boil, then turn the heat down, cover and simmer until the rice is cooked and the water absorbed, about 15 minutes. Remove from the heat and let stand, covered, until ready to serve.
2 While the rice is cooking, heat the olive oil in a large saucepan over medium heat. Fry the onion, garlic, ginger and spice powder 2 minutes, stirring constantly.
3 Stir in the coconut milk and stock. Add the shellfish and bring to a boil, then turn the heat down and add the lime juice, mango chutney, to taste, and ketchup. Stir well.
4 Season with salt and pepper, then simmer until the shellfish is cooked and the sauce has reduced and thickened, about 10 minutes. Sprinkle with parsley and serve with the rice.

< NEARLY CAESAR SALAD

An authentic Caesar salad contains anchovies. This is a delicious vegetarian variation.

4 eggs • 2 tablespoons extra-virgin olive oil • 2 thick slices of white bread, crusts removed and cubed • 2 garlic cloves • 1 handful of trimmed fine green beans • 2 romaine hearts, leaves separated • 2-ounce piece Parmesan cheese
DRESSING: 1 egg • juice of ½ small lemon • 1 garlic clove, halved • scant 1 cup sunflower oil • ¼ cup grated Parmesan cheese • salt and freshly ground black pepper

TO SERVE: lemon wedges and olive bread

1 Soft-cook the eggs 3 minutes. Let cool, then peel and cut into quarters.
2 Meanwhile, heat the olive oil in a large, nonstick frying pan over medium heat. Fry the bread with the garlic until golden, 2 to 3 minutes. Drain the croûtons on paper towels, season and let cool.
3 Blanch the beans in boiling water until just tender, about 2 minutes. Drain and rinse under cold water.
4 To make the dressing, put the egg in a food processor with the lemon juice and garlic and blend until smooth. With the motor running, slowly add the sunflower oil until the mixture starts to emulsify and thicken, then add the oil more quickly until it has all been incorporated. Add the grated Parmesan and season to taste.
5 Put the lettuce in a serving bowl and top with the beans, eggs and croûtons. Using a vegetable peeler, shave the Parmesan over the top and drizzle on the dressing. Serve with lemon wedges and slices of olive bread.

TWO-PEPPER PIPÉRADE

In this version of the well-known Basque dish, I think glorious runny egg yolks beat the more traditional scrambled version every time.

5 tablespoons olive oil • 1 large onion, sliced • 1 garlic clove, minced • 3 bell peppers (2 red and 1 yellow), seeded and thinly sliced • 8 cherry tomatoes, cut in half • 4 extra-large eggs • chili oil, for drizzling • salt and freshly ground black pepper

TO SERVE: ciabatta rolls and green salad

1 Heat the olive oil in a large, nonstick frying pan over medium heat. Fry the onion and garlic 2 minutes, then add the peppers and tomatoes. Cook, stirring regularly, until the peppers are softened, about 10 minutes. Season with salt and pepper.
2 Make four nests in the mixture and carefully break in the eggs. Cook until the whites of the eggs are just set but the yolks remain runny, 3 to 4 minutes.
3 Drizzle a little chili oil over and serve with ciabatta rolls and a green salad.

SWISS CHEESE FONDUE

Fondues are great fun and this one is simple to make. Bread is *de rigueur* as an accompaniment, but you could also try tiny boiled new potatoes. Tradition has it that anyone losing their bread in the fondue has to pay a forfeit!

1¼ cups fruity dry white wine • 1½ pounds Gruyère cheese, grated • 3 tablespoons kirsch or grappa • 1 teaspoon potato flour • 1 teaspoon thyme leaves (optional) • 1 garlic clove, cut in half • freshly ground black pepper

TO SERVE: French bread, cut into bite-size chunks

1 Heat the wine in a medium-size saucepan over medium heat until hot. Add the Gruyère and heat until the cheese has melted, stirring occasionally.
2 Meanwhile, mix the kirsch and potato flour together. Stir into the cheese mixture and cook until thickened, 3 to 4 minutes. Add the thyme, if using, and season with plenty of black pepper.
3 Rub the cut sides of the garlic around the inside of the fondue pot and set it over its burner. Pour the cheese fondue into the pot and serve with chunks of French bread for dunking.

POLENTA WITH ARTICHOKE SAUCE

This is a rich and tasty dish that artichoke fans will love. Choose good artichokes in olive oil over those in water or vinegar.

1 cup mascarpone cheese • 3 tablespoons milk • ½ cup grated Parmesan cheese • 1¼ pounds jarred artichokes in olive oil, drained • 2 teaspoons thyme leaves
POLENTA: 2¼ cups instant polenta • 8 cups vegetable stock • ½ cup grated Parmesan cheese • 1 handful of parsley, leaves chopped • salt and freshly ground black pepper

1 Make the polenta following the directions on the package, using the vegetable stock instead of water. When the polenta has thickened, stir in the Parmesan and parsley, then season with salt and pepper.
2 Meanwhile, put the mascarpone in a saucepan with the milk and Parmesan. Stir over low heat until smooth, about 2 minutes.
3 Add half of the artichokes to the mascarpone mixture and, using a hand blender, blend to a fairly smooth purée. Add the remaining artichokes and the thyme and stir over low heat until heated through. Season with plenty of pepper.
4 Pile the polenta into a serving dish and top with the artichoke sauce. Serve hot.

BEAN CHILE WITH AVOCADO CREAM

This delicious meat-free chile is a great pantry meal that is made even better with the avocado cream accompaniment.

3 tablespoons olive oil • 1 onion, chopped • 1 teaspoon ground cumin • 1 teaspooon ground coriander • 1 teaspoon hot chili powder, plus extra to taste • 14 ounces canned cherry tomatoes • 1 teaspoon sugar • 14 ounces canned red kidney beans, drained and rinsed • 14 ounces canned cannellini beans, drained and rinsed • 14 ounces canned black-eyed peas, drained and rinsed • 1 handful of cilantro, leaves chopped • salt and freshly ground black pepper
AVOCADO CREAM: 2 ripe avocados, pitted and roughly chopped • 6 tablespoons sour cream

TO SERVE: tortillas and green salad

1 Heat the olive oil in a large saucepan over medium heat. Fry the onion and spices, stirring regularly, until softened, 2 to 3 minutes.
2 Stir in the cherry tomatoes, sugar and beans. Bring to a boil, then turn the heat down and simmer until reduced and thickened, about 15 minutes. Season with salt and pepper, then stir in three-fourths of the cilantro. Taste and add extra chili powder if you want more heat.
3 While the chile is simmering, blend the avocado with the sour cream until smooth. Season to taste and spoon into a bowl.
4 Scatter the remaining cilantro over the chile and serve with the avocado cream, tortillas and a salad of mixed greens.

BROCCOLI RAAB WITH ORECCHIETTE >

Fans of slightly bitter vegetables will love the way broccoli raab complements the almost buttery flavor of the orecchiette pasta and toasted hazelnuts in this traditional southern Italian dish. Called *cima di rapa* in Italy, you can substitute other slightly bitter greens, such as turnip or mustard greens or kale, if you can't find it.

1 pound dried orecchiette pasta • 3 tablespoons olive oil • 2 garlic cloves, thinly sliced • 1¼ pounds broccoli raab, tough stems discarded, roughly chopped • juice of 1 small lemon • 1 handful of toasted hazelnuts, lightly chopped • salt and freshly ground black pepper

TO SERVE: lemon wedges and green salad

1 Bring a large saucepan of salted water to a boil and cook the orecchiette until almost al dente, about 2 minutes less than directed on the package.
2 Meanwhile, heat the olive oil in a large, nonstick frying pan over medium heat. Fry the garlic 1 minute. Add the broccoli raab and fry until the leaves have wilted, 3 to 4 minutes.
3 Add the lemon juice and season with salt and pepper. Cook until the broccoli raab stalks have softened, 3 to 4 minutes.
4 Using a slotted spoon, transfer the pasta to the pan with the broccoli raab. Stir and cook until the pasta absorbs the lemony flavours and is al dente, about 2 minutes.
5 Scatter the hazelnuts over the pasta and serve with lemon wedges and a salad of mixed greens.

WALNUT PESTO LINGUINE

If you have trouble finding walnut oil, extra-virgin olive oil is fine in its place. Be careful not to over-process the walnuts or they will become too oily and lose their crunchy texture and flavor.

1 pound dried linguine • 2 garlic cloves, peeled • 1 cup grated Parmesan cheese, plus extra for serving • 1 cup walnut halves • 4 to 5 tablespoons walnut oil • 1 small handful of parsley, leaves chopped • salt and freshly ground black pepper

TO SERVE: arugula, watercress and spinach salad

1 Bring a large saucepan of salted water to a boil and cook the linguine until al dente, 10 to 12 minutes.
2 Meanwhile, put the garlic, Parmesan and walnuts in a food processer and blitz to a coarse paste. Stir in the walnut oil and parsley, then season with salt and pepper.
3 Drain the linguine and toss with the pesto. Serve with extra grated Parmesan and an arugula, watercress and spinach salad.

WHO'D HAVE THOUGHT THAT IN LESS THAN THIRTY MINUTES IT'S POSSIBLE TO ROAST RED MULLET AND SERVE IT WITH A CHILI AND GARLIC VINAIGRETTE, BAKE A CHERRY TOMATO CLAFOUTIS, OR RUSTLE UP A THAI CHICKEN CURRY? HERE ARE DISHES THAT MAKE GREAT FAMILY MEALS, YET WILL ALSO GO DOWN WELL AT ANY DINNER PARTY.

TWENTY-FIVE- MINUTE MEALS

THAI CHICKEN CURRY

I've used a red Thai curry paste here, but green works well too, so don't be afraid to experiment.

2 tablespoons olive oil • 1 onion, chopped • 2 garlic cloves, chopped • 1 pound skinless, boneless chicken breasts or thighs, cut into bite-size pieces • 2 tablespoons Thai red curry paste • 2 teaspoons sugar • 1 teaspoon fish sauce • 1¾ cups canned coconut milk • 2 kaffir lime leaves, shredded • 1¼ cups jasmine rice • salt and freshly ground black pepper

1 Heat the olive oil in a large, heavy-based saucepan over medium heat. Fry the onion and garlic until softened, about 2 minutes.
2 Add the chicken and cook, turning occasionally, until browned, 3 to 4 minutes. Stir in the curry paste, sugar, fish sauce and coconut milk, and season with salt and pepper.
3 Bring to a boil, then turn the heat down and simmer until the chicken is cooked through, about 15 minutes. Stir in the kaffir lime leaves.
4 While the chicken is simmering, put the rice in a medium-size pan and cover with 2½ cups water. Bring to a boil, then turn the heat down, cover and simmer until the rice is cooked and the water absorbed, 10 to 12 minutes. Remove from the heat and let stand, covered, until ready to serve.
5 Using a fork, fluff up the rice and serve with the chicken curry.

GOLDEN CHICKEN GOUJONS WITH MAYO

Crisp chicken goujons marry beautifully with this herb and garlic mayonnaise.

1 pound small new potatoes • ⅓ cup olive oil • ½ teaspoon dried oregano • 2 garlic cloves, peeled • 1 pound skinless, boneless chicken breast halves • ½ cup grated Parmesan cheese • 4 tablespoons dry white bread crumbs • 1 egg, beaten • salt and freshly ground black pepper
HERB & GARLIC MAYONNAISE: 1 egg • 2 tablespoons white wine vinegar • 2 garlic cloves, peeled • scant 1 cup sunflower oil • 1 handful of mixed herbs (chives, parsley and basil), leaves chopped

TO SERVE: green salad

1 Put the potatoes in a saucepan with half the olive oil and the oregano. Cover and cook over medium heat until soft and golden, about 20 minutes.
2 Meanwhile, make the mayonnaise following the instructions on page 98, replacing the lemon juice with vinegar and adding garlic instead of mustard. Transfer to a bowl, stir in the herbs and season.
3 To prepare the chicken, pound the garlic into a paste with a large pinch of salt and pepper. Rub the mixture over the chicken, then cut it into strips.
4 Mix the Parmesan and bread crumbs together on a plate. Dip the chicken pieces into the egg, then coat with the bread crumbs.
5 Heat the remaining oil in a large, nonstick frying pan over medium heat. Fry the chicken, in two batches, until golden and cooked through, 5 to 6 minutes. Serve hot with the mayonnaise, new potatoes and a salad of mixed greens.

CHEESY CHICKEN WRAPPED IN PANCETTA

1 pound sweet potatoes, peeled and cut into small chunks • ¼ stick butter • 4 skinless, boneless chicken breast halves, each about 6 ounces • 4 ounces sharp Cheddar cheese or similar, cut into 4 long slices • 8 long slices of pancetta or bacon • 3 tablespoons olive oil • 2¼ pounds spinach leaves, washed • salt and freshly ground black pepper

1 Cook the sweet potatoes in a pan of boiling salted water until tender, 15 to 20 minutes; drain and mash, then stir in the butter.

2 While the potatoes are cooking, cut a pocket in each chicken breast and insert a slice of cheese. Wrap two slices of pancetta around each chicken breast to cover completely.

3 Heat the olive oil in a large, nonstick frying pan over medium heat. Fry the chicken breasts until the pancetta is golden and the chicken is cooked through, about 10 minutes per side.

4 At the same time, cook the spinach in a pan, with only the water clinging to the leaves after washing, until wilted, 2 to 3 minutes; season to taste. Serve the chicken with the sweet potatoes and spinach.

PORK TONNATO

This is a variation on the classic Italian dish *vitello tonnato*—veal in a delicious, creamy tuna mayonnaise sauce. It makes a delightful dinner.

1 pound new potatoes • 1 tablespoon butter
• 4 pork cutlets, each about 6 ounces
• 2 tablespoons olive oil • 6 sage leaves
• 1 tablespoon salted capers, rinsed and drained
• 1 handful of parsley, leaves chopped • salt and freshly ground black pepper
TUNA SAUCE: 1 egg • juice of ½ small lemon
• 1 cup sunflower oil • 4 to 5 ounces canned or jarred tuna in olive oil, drained

TO SERVE: lemon wedges and quartered romaine hearts

1 Cook the potatoes in a saucepan of boiling salted water until tender, 15 to 20 minutes; drain and toss with the butter.
2 Meanwhile, to make the tuna sauce, put the egg in a food processor with the lemon juice and a little salt and pepper. Blend a few seconds until smooth. With the motor running, slowly trickle in the sunflower oil a little at a time. When the mixture starts to emulsify and thicken, add the oil more quickly. Once it has all been incorporated, add the tuna and blend briefly until combined.
3 Season the pork to taste. Heat the olive oil in a large, nonstick frying pan over medium heat. Fry the pork with the sage until cooked through and golden, about 4 minutes per side. Transfer the pork to a serving platter.
4 Spoon the tuna sauce over the pork and top with the capers and parsley. Season with a little more pepper and serve with lemon wedges, new potatoes and wedges of romaine.

PORK WITH PRUNES

These juicy nuggets of pork are served in a creamy sauce with sweet prunes. I like to use the plump, moist variety because of their slight chewiness, but canned prunes are fine, too.

1¼ cups long-grain rice • 1 tablespoon olive oil
• 2 shallots, minced • 2 garlic cloves, minced
• 8 small sage leaves • 1 pound pork tenderloin, sliced • ½ cup dry white wine • 1 large handful of prunes • 1 tablespoon wholegrain mustard • ⅔ cup heavy cream • 4 handfuls of sugar snap peas • salt and freshly ground black pepper

1 Put the rice in a medium-size saucepan and cover with 2½ cups water. Bring to a boil, then turn the heat down, cover and simmer until the rice is cooked and the water absorbed, about 15 minutes. Remove from the heat and let stand, covered, until ready to serve.
2 While the rice is cooking, heat the olive oil in a large, nonstick frying pan over medium heat. Fry the shallots, garlic and sage until softened, about 2 minutes. Add the pork slices and cook, turning occasionally, until golden, about 6 minutes.
3 Pour the wine into the pan, turn the heat down and add the prunes and mustard. Simmer 2 minutes, stirring occasionally, then add the cream and season with salt and pepper. Simmer, stirring often, until the cream has reduced and thickened, about 3 minutes.
4 At the same time, cook the sugar snap peas in boiling salted water until tender but still crisp, 2 to 3 minutes; drain. Serve the pork with the rice and sugar snap peas.

GRILLED HAM STEAKS WITH PINEAPPLE & MINT RELISH

Salty ham and sweet, juicy pineapple are a classic combination, but add chopped mint and serve with chili-spiked potatoes and you have a very special dish.

5 tablespoons olive oil • 1 pound baby new potatoes, quartered • 1 dried chili (mildly hot or hot, to taste), crumbled • 4 ham steaks, each about 6 ounces • 4 handfuls of sugar snap peas • salt and freshly ground black pepper
PINEAPPLE & MINT RELISH: 1 small pineapple, peeled, cored and roughly chopped • 2 shallots, chopped • 1 tablespoon extra-virgin olive oil • 1 small handful of mint, leaves shredded

1 Heat 4 tablespoons of the olive oil in a large, nonstick frying pan over medium heat. Sauté the potatoes with the chili, turning occasionally, until tender and golden, 15 to 20 minutes. Drain on paper towels and season with salt and pepper.
2 Meanwhile, make the pineapple and mint relish. Put the pineapple in a bowl and stir in the shallots, olive oil, mint and a little black pepper. Set aside.
3 Brush the ham steaks with the remaining oil. Heat a ridged grill pan over medium-high heat. Grill the ham steaks until cooked, 4 to 5 minutes per side.
4 Steam the sugar snap peas until just tender, 2 to 3 minutes. Serve the ham steaks topped with a generous spoonful of pineapple relish, and the chili potatoes and sugar snap peas on the side.

HERB SAUSAGE PATTIES WITH CHILI GREENS

If you can't find fresh bulk pork sausage, simply slip meaty pork link sausages out of their skins. This dish goes well with baked beans.

1¾ pounds fresh pork sausage • 1 onion, minced • 1 teaspoon dried oregano • 2 tablespoons olive oil • 2 garlic cloves, chopped • 1 dried chili (mildly hot or hot, to taste), crumbled • 1¾ pounds cooking greens, such as kale or collard greens, roughly chopped • juice of 1 lime (optional) • salt and freshly ground black pepper

TO SERVE: baked beans or crusty bread

1 Preheat the broiler.
2 Put the sausage in a large bowl and add the onion and oregano. Knead until combined, then divide the mixture into eight and form into patties about ½-inch thick.
3 Broil the sausage patties until cooked through, about 4 minutes per side.
4 Meanwhile, heat the olive oil in a large, nonstick frying pan over medium heat. Fry the garlic and chili 1 minute, stirring to infuse the oil with their flavors. Add the greens and cook until tender and wilted, about 3 minutes. Squeeze in the lime juice, if using, and season with salt and pepper.
5 Serve the sausage patties hot with the chili greens and baked beans or crusty bread.

STICKY LAMB SATAY

Lamb works well with the rich, peanut satay sauce. You will need 12 metal skewers.

1 pound boneless lamb, cut into 12 thin strips • 9 ounces dried egg noodles • 1 handful of cilantro, chopped
MARINADE: 1 garlic clove, minced • 1-inch piece fresh ginger root, peeled and chopped • 1 tablespoon honey • 1 teaspoon fish sauce • juice of 1 lime
SATAY SAUCE: ½ cup crunchy peanut butter • ½ cup canned coconut milk • 1 to 2 tablespoons chili sauce • 1 garlic clove, minced • 1 tablespoon dark soy sauce

TO SERVE: spinach salad

1 Thread the lamb onto 12 skewers and place in a shallow dish. Mix together all the ingredients for the marinade and pour it over the lamb, turning until coated. Let marinate 10 minutes.
2 Meanwhile, preheat the broiler. Mix together all the ingredients for the satay sauce until combined, then set aside.
3 Broil the lamb until golden brown, 3 to 4 minutes per side. (Discard the leftover marinade.)
4 At the same time, bring a pan of salted water to a boil and cook the noodles until soft, 3 to 4 minutes; drain. Sprinkle the cilantro over the lamb and serve with the noodles, satay sauce and a spinach salad.

PICADILLO WITH AVOCADO SALSA

This is my version of the spiced ground beef dish that is popular in many Latin American countries. It's often used as a filling for tortillas and tacos, which is how I like to serve it, along with a lip-smacking avocado salsa.

2 tablespoons olive oil • 2 garlic cloves, minced • 1 onion, chopped • 1 pound lean ground beef • 14 ounces canned crushed tomatoes • ½ cup white wine • 3 to 4 pickled jalapeño peppers, chopped • 1 handful of pitted green olives • 4 taco shells • salt and freshly ground black pepper

AVOCADO SALSA: 2 ripe avocados, pitted and diced • 1 large tomato, seeded and diced • 1 small red onion, minced • 1 small handful of cilantro, chopped • juice of 1 lime

1 Heat the olive oil in a large, nonstick frying pan over medium heat. Fry the garlic and onion until softened, about 2 minutes. Add the beef and cook, stirring often, until browned, 3 to 4 minutes.

2 Stir in the tomatoes, wine, jalapeños and olives. Season with salt and pepper. Bring to a boil, then turn the heat down and simmer until reduced and thickened, about 15 minutes.

3 Meanwhile, preheat the oven to 350°F. Mix together the ingredients for the avocado salsa and season to taste.

4 Place the tacos on a baking sheet and warm through in the oven 5 minutes. Spoon the picadillo into the tacos and serve with the salsa.

SPICED BEEF & BEAN THREADS SALAD >

Although I've suggested serving the beef hot in this recipe, it is also really nice served at room temperature, so it's perfect for a summer meal.

2 tablespoons dark soy sauce • 1 tablespoon fish sauce • 1 to 2 tablespoon chili sauce • 1 garlic clove, minced • 2 handfuls of salted peanuts, roughly chopped • 1 pound lean steak, cut into strips • 2 tablespoons olive oil • 1 small handful of cilantro leaves
BEAN THREADS SALAD: 4 ounces dried bean threads (cellophane noodles) • 1 handful of trimmed fine green beans • 1 tablespoon honey • juice of 1 lime • 3 tablespoons olive oil • 1 tablespoon fish sauce • 1 handful of snow peas • 3 scallions, sliced diagonally • salt

1 To make the salad, bring a pan of salted water to a boil and cook the noodles until soft, 3 to 4 minutes. Drain and rinse in cold water; transfer to a bowl.
2 Meanwhile, blanch the beans in boiling water 2 minutes, then drain and rinse in cold water. Mix together the honey, lime juice, olive oil and fish sauce until combined. Add the beans to the noodles along with the snow peas and scallions. Pour the dressing over and toss well.
3 Mix together the soy sauce, fish sauce, chili sauce and garlic in a bowl. Put the peanuts in a separate bowl. Turn the beef in the soy mixture, then press the meat firmly into the peanuts to coat.
4 Heat the olive oil in a wok or large, nonstick frying pan over medium-high heat. Stir-fry the beef until the peanut coating is golden, 4 to 5 minutes.
5 Scatter the cilantro over the noodles and beef before serving.

VEAL CHOPS IN SAGE & RED WINE

This great dinner-party dish also works well with pork chops.

4 tablespoons olive oil • 1 pound baby new potatoes, cut in half • 3 garlic cloves, sliced • 1 small handful of small sage leaves • 4 veal chops • 1 cup red wine • 4 handfuls of snow peas • salt and freshly ground black pepper

1 Heat half the olive oil in a large, nonstick frying pan over medium heat. Sauté the potatoes, turning occasionally, until tender and golden, about 15 to 20 minutes. Season with salt and pepper.
2 Meanwhile, heat the remaining oil in another large, nonstick frying pan over medium-low heat. Fry the garlic and sage leaves 2 minutes, stirring often.
3 Season the veal and place in the pan with the garlic and sage. Turn the heat up a little and fry the veal until browned and cooked, about 5 minutes per side. Pour in the red wine and bubble until reduced, 4 to 5 minutes.
4 At the same time, steam the snow peas until just tender, 2 to 3 minutes. Serve the veal chops with the sautéed potatoes and snow peas.

LEMON & OLIVE ROASTED FISH

The secret to this succulent roasted fish dish is a very hot oven. Other than that, the preparation is incredibly simple and quick. Ask your fish merchant to prepare the fish for you.

4 (1- to 1½-pound) whole red porgy or gray snapper, cleaned and scaled if necessary • 4 tablespoons extra-virgin olive oil • juice of 1 small lemon • 1 lemon, cut into wedges • 3 to 4 thyme sprigs • 1 handful of pitted black olives • 1 pound broccolini
LEMON & PARSLEY QUINOA: 1¼ cups quinoa • grated zest and juice of 1 lemon • 1 handful of parsley, leaves chopped • salt and freshly ground black pepper

1 Preheat the oven to 425°F.
2 Place the fish side by side in a baking dish and make three cuts in the top side of each fish. Brush the fish with the olive oil.
3 Squeeze a little lemon juice over the fish, then arrange the remaining wedges on top. Scatter the thyme and olives over, then season with salt and pepper. Roast until cooked, about 20 minutes.
4 Meanwhile, put the quinoa in a pan and cover with water. Bring to a boil, then reduce the heat to low, cover and simmer until tender, about 10 minutes. Drain well. Toss the quinoa with the lemon zest and juice and the parsley, then season.
5 At the same time, steam the broccolini until just tender, 4 to 5 minutes. Serve the fish hot with the broccolini and quinoa.

< BLACKENED FISH WITH TZATZIKI

This is a fabulous way to prepare white fish. The lime and tzatziki create a wonderfully cooling accompaniment to the spiciness of the fish.

1 pound new potatoes, halved • 2 garlic cloves, peeled • 1 tablespoon freshly ground black pepper, plus extra to taste • 1 tablespoon dried oregano • 1 tablespoon thyme leaves • 1 teaspoon cayenne or hot chili powder • ½ stick butter • 4 firm white fish fillets, each about 6 ounces
TZATZIKI: 1¼ cups thick Greek yogurt • 1 small hothouse cucumber, peeled, seeded and diced • salt and freshly ground black pepper

TO SERVE: lime wedges and green salad

1 Cook the potatoes in a saucepan of boiling salted water until tender, 15 to 20 minutes; drain.
2 Meanwhile, sprinkle a little salt over the garlic and work it to a paste using the flat blade of a large knife. Put the garlic paste in a bowl and add the black pepper. Stir in the herbs and cayenne.
3 Heat the butter in a large, nonstick frying pan over high heat. Brush the top of the fish fillets with some of the butter and scatter the spice mix over to coat. Fry the fish in the butter remaining in the pan—spice-side down first—until blackened and crisp, about 3 minutes, then turn the fillets over and fry 3 minutes longer.
4 Spoon the yogurt into a serving bowl. Stir in the cucumber and season to taste. Serve the fish with the tzatziki, new potatoes, a salad of mixed greens and lime wedges.

ROASTED RED MULLET WITH CHILI & GARLIC VINAIGRETTE >

Look for imported red mullet in ethnic fish markets; if you cannot find it use red snapper instead. With small fish, you will need four.

2 large red mullet, cleaned and scaled • 2 lemons • 2 sweet potatoes, peeled and diced • 2 tablespoons olive oil • 4 cups sugar snap peas • salt and freshly ground black pepper
CHILI & GARLIC VINAIGRETTE: 1 small dried chili (mildly hot or hot, to taste) • ½ cup extra-virgin olive oil • 2 garlic cloves, sliced • 2 tablespoons minced sun-dried tomatoes • 1 tablespoon wholegrain mustard • 2 tablespoons ketchup

1 Preheat the oven to 425°F.
2 Lay the fish in a large baking dish and make two cuts in the top side of each fish. Cut one of the lemons into wedges and arrange around the fish with the sweet potatoes. Drizzle the olive oil over the fish and squeeze a little lemon juice from the second lemon over them. Season with salt and pepper, then roast until the fish is cooked and the sweet potatoes are tender, about 20 minutes.
3 Meanwhile, make the dressing: Toast the chili in a frying pan until slightly charred, about 1 minute. Add the olive oil, garlic and sun-dried tomatoes, then cook over low heat 3 to 4 minutes. Stir in the mustard and ketchup, the remaining lemon juice, and salt and pepper to taste.
4 Steam the sugar snap peas until just tender, 2 to 3 minutes. Spoon the vinaigrette over the fish and serve with the sweet potatoes and sugar snap peas.

MOROCCAN-SPICED FISH WITH COUSCOUS

Spice-coated fish makes a great match with buttery, saffron-flecked couscous.

1⅔ cups couscous • pinch of saffron threads • 2 cups hot vegetable or chicken stock • ½ preserved lemon, chopped • 1 handful of toasted sliced almonds • 1 handful of golden raisins • ¾ stick butter • 2 tablespoons cilantro seeds • 2 tablespoons cumin seeds • 2 teaspoons ground cinnamon • 1 garlic clove, minced • 5 to 6 tablespoons olive oil • 4 pollock fillets (or fillets of other fish), each about 7 ounces • 1 handful of cilantro, chopped • salt and freshly ground black pepper

TO SERVE: tomato and arugula salad

1 Preheat the oven to 400°F.
2 Put the couscous in a baking dish and stir in the saffron. Pour the hot stock over and stir. Cover and let stand 4 to 5 minutes. Stir in the preserved lemon, almonds and raisins; season with salt and pepper. Dot half of the butter over the top and bake until heated through, about 10 minutes.
3 Meanwhile, toast the whole spices in a frying pan until fragrant, about 2 minutes. Using a pestle and mortar, grind them to a powder, then stir in the cinnamon, garlic and 2 to 3 tablespoons of the olive oil to make a thick but spreadable paste. Smear the mixture over the fish fillets.
4 Heat the remaining oil in a large, nonstick frying pan over medium-high heat. Fry the fish until cooked and crisp, 4 to 5 minutes per side.
5 Remove the couscous from the oven and stir in the remaining butter and the cilantro. Serve the fish with the couscous and a tomato and arugula salad.

PARMESAN-CRUSTED COD WITH BUTTERED CORN

Buttery puréed corn is absolutely delicious—
it lifts frozen corn to new heights.

2 tablespoons all-purpose flour • ½ cup grated
Parmesan cheese • 2 tablespoons minced chives
• 4 skinless cod fillets, each about 6 ounces • 1 egg
white, beaten • 4 tablespoons olive oil • 1 pound
fresh penne pasta • ¼ stick butter • salt and freshly
ground black pepper
BUTTERED CORN: 2 cups frozen corn kernels
• 1 bay leaf • ¼ teaspoon sugar • ¼ stick butter

1 To make the buttered corn, put the corn kernels in
a saucepan with the bay leaf and add enough water
just to cover. Bring to a boil, then turn the heat down
and simmer until soft, 3 to 4 minutes.
2 Meanwhile, mix the flour, Parmesan, chives and
some seasoning together on a plate; set aside.
3 Drain the corn and transfer to a blender,
discarding the bay leaf. Add the sugar and blend
until coarse-fine. Return the corn mixture to the pan
and add the butter, season with salt and pepper,
then warm through.
4 Dip the fish into the egg white, then dust in the
Parmesan mixture to coat. Heat the olive oil in
a large, nonstick frying pan over medium heat.
Fry the fish until cooked and golden, about
4 minutes per side.
5 At the same time, bring a large saucepan of
salted water to a boil and cook the penne until al
dente, about 2 minutes. Drain, then toss with the
butter. Serve the fish with the corn and penne.

SALMON IN LEMONY BUTTER SAUCE

This rich, lemony sauce makes a heavenly
accompaniment for succulent salmon fillets,
but it's another one of those adaptable sauces
that marries well with white fish, too.

1 pound new potatoes • 4 salmon fillets, each
about 6 ounces • 2 tablespoons olive oil • juice
of ½ lemon • 3 cups frozen petite peas • salt and
freshly ground black pepper
LEMONY BUTTER SAUCE: juice of 1 small lemon
• 3 tablespoons heavy cream • 1½ sticks butter,
diced • 1 handful of parsley, leaves chopped

1 Preheat the oven to 400°F. Cook the potatoes
in a saucepan of boiling salted water until tender,
15 to 20 minutes; drain.
2 Meanwhile, season the salmon with salt and
pepper. Heat the olive oil in a large, nonstick frying
pan over high heat. Fry the salmon 2 minutes on
each side, then transfer to a roasting pan. Squeeze
the lemon juice over the fish and bake until just
cooked but still slightly opaque in the center, about
6 minutes.
3 To make the sauce, put the lemon juice in a small
pan and add the cream and 2 tablespoons water.
Set the pan over low heat. Add the butter, a little
at a time, stirring well. When it has all been
incorporated, the sauce will be thick and creamy.
Stir in the parsley and season to taste.
4 Cook the peas in boiling salted water until tender,
3 to 4 minutes, then drain. Serve the salmon with
the sauce spooned over and the potatoes and
peas alongside.

PEPPER-CRUSTED TUNA WITH BEAN COMPÔTE

Tuna has a meaty texture that works really well with this crunchy peppercorn coating. The sugar tempers the heat of the pepper a little, so don't be tempted to leave it out.

1⅔ cups couscous • 2 cups hot vegetable stock • 4 handfuls of trimmed fine green beans • 1 handful of cherry tomatoes, cut in half • 1 handful of pitted black olives • 2 garlic cloves, minced • ½ cup olive oil • 2 tablespoons balsamic vinegar • 4 tuna steaks, each about 7 ounces • 2 tablespoons coarsely ground black peppercorns • 1 teaspoon brown sugar

1 Put the couscous in a bowl and pour the hot stock over. Stir, then cover and let stand until the stock is absorbed, 5 to 6 minutes. Fluff up the couscous with a fork, then set aside, covered.

2 While the couscous is soaking, blanch the beans in boiling salted water 2 minutes. Drain and rinse under cold running water. Transfer to a saucepan and stir in the tomatoes, olives and garlic. Pour in 6 tablespoons of the olive oil and the balsamic vinegar, then let warm over low heat 4 to 5 minutes.

3 Meanwhile, brush the tuna steaks with a little of the remaining olive oil. Mix the coarsely ground peppercorns and sugar together and press firmly over both sides of the tuna to coat.

4 Heat the rest of the oil in a ridged grill pan over medium-high heat. Grill the tuna until seared but still slightly pink in the center, about 2 minutes per side (the exact cooking time will depend on the thickness of the steaks). Serve the tuna with the bean compôte and couscous.

BAKED SEA BASS IN NEWSPAPER

Cooking fish in a newspaper or baking paper package keeps it moist and succulent, and much of the skin comes away as the fish is unwrapped. You will need four sheets of newspaper in total.

4 small whole sea bass, cleaned and scaled
• 1 pound trimmed green beans
DRESSING: ½ cup extra-virgin olive oil • 1 large, ripe tomato, seeded and roughly chopped
• 2 tablespoons minced fennel bulb • 1 shallot, minced • 1 garlic clove, minced • finely grated zest and juice of 1 lime • 1 small dried chili (mildly hot or hot, to taste; optional) • salt and freshly ground black pepper

TO SERVE: crusty bread

1 Preheat the oven to 450°F.
2 Carefully dampen four sheets of newspaper and wrap one fish in each. Place the packages in a roasting pan and bake until the fish is cooked, about 20 minutes.
3 Meanwhile, cook the green beans in boiling salted water until tender, 4 to 5 minutes; drain.
4 To make the dressing, pour the oil into a small saucepan. Stir in the tomato, fennel, shallot, garlic, and lime zest and juice, and crumble in the chili, if using. Season with salt and pepper and heat gently until warm. Pour the dressing into a small pitcher.
5 Serve the fish, still wrapped in newspaper, so that diners can open their packages at the table and help themselves to the dressing. Serve with the green beans and slices of crusty bread.

FISH KOFTAS WITH COCONUT RICE

Spicy, delicious and so easy to make, these skewers of ground fish also make great barbecue food. You will need 8 metal skewers.

1 tablespoon cilantro seeds • 1 tablespoon cumin seeds • 9 ounces skinless white fish fillets
• 9 ounces peeled raw shrimp • 1 teaspoon ground cinnamon • 1 teaspoon ground ginger • 1 garlic clove, peeled • finely grated zest of 1 lemon
• 1 teaspoon brown sugar • 2 tablespoons dried shredded coconut • 2 tablespoons olive oil • salt
COCONUT RICE: 1¼ cups basmati rice
• 1¾ cups canned coconut milk

TO SERVE: green salad

1 Put the rice in a medium-size saucepan with the coconut milk and scant 1 cup water. Bring to a boil, then turn the heat down, cover and simmer until the rice is cooked and the liquid absorbed, about 15 minutes. Remove from the heat and let stand, covered, until ready to serve.
2 While the rice is cooking, toast the whole spices in a frying pan until fragrant, 2 to 3 minutes. Using a pestle and mortar, grind them into a powder.
3 Put the fish and shrimp in a food processor and add the ground spices and garlic. Blitz to a coarse paste, then spoon the mixture into a bowl. Stir in the lemon zest, sugar and coconut. Season with salt. Form the mixture into eight sausage-shaped koftas around the skewers.
4 Heat the olive oil in a large, nonstick frying pan over medium heat. Fry the koftas, turning, until golden, 6 to 7 minutes. Serve with the coconut rice and a salad of mixed greens.

LINGUINE WITH CLAMS & WHITE WINE

This is my version of spaghetti vongole—one of my absolute favorite classic Italian dishes. The recipe works beautifully with mussels, too.

14 ounces dried linguine pasta • 2 tablespoons olive oil • 3 shallots, minced • 2 garlic cloves, sliced • 2¼ pounds littleneck clams, scrubbed and rinsed well • ½ cup dry white wine • 1 handful of parsley, leaves chopped

TO SERVE: tomato and red basil salad

1 Bring a large saucepan of salted water to a boil and cook the linguine until almost al dente, about 2 minutes less than the directions on the package.
2 Meanwhile, heat the olive oil in a large, deep frying pan over medium-low heat. Fry the shallots and garlic 2 minutes, then add the clams.
3 Turn the heat up, stir and add the wine. Cover with a lid and cook until the clams have opened, about 5 minutes. Discard any that remain closed.
4 Drain the linguine and transfer to the pan with the clams. Cook over low heat 2 minutes, stirring occasionally. Stir in the parsley and serve with a tomato and red basil salad.

FIG, LENTIL & FETA SALAD

Fresh figs have a fantastic affinity with lentils and salty feta. Goat cheese works very well, too.

1½ cups Puy lentils • 4 tablespoons extra-virgin olive oil • 1 onion, chopped • 1 garlic clove, minced • 1 teaspoon minced rosemary • 3 tablespoons balsamic vinegar • 3 ripe figs, cut into bite-size pieces • 9 ounces feta cheese, crumbled • salt and freshly ground black pepper

TO SERVE: arugula salad and crusty bread

1 Cook the lentils in boiling water until tender, about 20 minutes.
2 Meanwhile, heat 2 tablespoons of the olive oil in a saucepan over medium heat. Fry the onion, garlic and rosemary until softened, about 2 minutes.
3 Drain the cooked lentils and add them to the pan with the onion. Stir in the balsamic vinegar and remaining oil. Season with salt and pepper.
4 Scatter the figs and feta over the lentils. Season with a little extra pepper and serve warm, with an arugula salad and slices of crusty bread.

FETA & CORN FRITTERS WITH SALSA >

These tasty fritters are always popular, with the salsa adding a real lift.

2 cups frozen corn kernels, thawed • 3 eggs, separated • 1 red onion, minced • 2 tablespoons chopped chives • ⅓ cup self-rising flour • 5½ ounces feta cheese, crumbled • ¼ stick butter
SALSA: 1 avocado, pitted and diced • 1 mango, pitted and diced • 1 papaya, seeded and diced • 1 red onion, chopped • 1 red bell pepper, seeded and diced • juice of 1 lime • 1 handful of cilantro, chopped • salt and freshly ground black pepper

TO SERVE: lime wedges and green salad

1 Put the corn in a large bowl. Add the egg yolks, red onion and chives, then stir in the flour and feta. Season with salt and pepper.
2 Beat the egg whites until they form stiff peaks, then fold them gently but thoroughly into the corn mixture.
3 Melt one-third of the butter in a large, nonstick frying pan over medium heat. Place four generous tablespoons of the batter in the pan, leaving a little space between each one, and cook until golden, 2 to 3 minutes per side. Remove the fritters from the pan and keep warm while you make more fritters using the rest of the batter and butter, to make 12 fritters in total.
4 Meanwhile, make the fruit salsa: Combine all the ingredients in a bowl and season to taste.
5 Serve three fritters per person with lime wedges for squeezing over, the fruit salsa and a salad.

SAVORY CORN TARTLETS

1 tablespoon butter, plus extra for greasing • 1 pound new potatoes • 1 sheet puff pastry, about 8 ounces, thawed if frozen • 2 eggs • 3 tablespoons mascarpone cheese • ¼ cup grated Parmesan cheese • 1 cup frozen corn kernels, thawed • 1 teaspoon thyme leaves • 1 pound broccoli florets • salt and freshly ground black pepper

1 Preheat the oven to 425°F and lightly grease a 12-cup muffin top pan.
2 Cook the potatoes in boiling water until tender, 15 to 20 minutes; drain and toss with the butter.
3 Meanwhile, cut disks from the sheet of pastry and use to line the muffin cups.
4 Beat the eggs and mascarpone in a large bowl until smooth, then stir in the Parmesan, corn, thyme and seasoning. Spoon into the tart shells and bake until the pastry is cooked, 8 to 10 minutes.
5 While the tarts are baking, steam the broccoli until just tender, about 5 minutes. Serve the tarts with the new potatoes and broccoli.

CHEESY SWEET POTATOES

This delicious, meat-free dish is rich and warming for chilly winter nights. If you can't find Taleggio, try another good melting cheese, such as French Reblochon, or the Irish Gubbeen.

2¼ pounds sweet potatoes, peeled and diced • 2½ cups heavy cream • 2 garlic cloves, peeled • 2 tablespoons thyme leaves • 7 ounces Taleggio cheese, cut into bite-size pieces • salt and freshly ground black pepper

TO SERVE: watercress, arugula and spinach salad

1 Cook the sweet potatoes in boiling, salted water until tender, 10 to 15 minutes.
2 Preheat the broiler.
3 Pour the cream into a heavy-based saucepan and add the garlic, thyme, a pinch of salt and a grinding of black pepper. Bring to a boil.
4 Drain the potatoes and spoon them into a large gratin dish or shallow oven-to-table dish. Scatter the Taleggio over the potatoes and pour the cream mixture over to coat.
5 Season with a little extra pepper, then broil, 3 to 4 inches from the heat, until bubbling and light golden, 3 to 4 minutes. Serve with a watercress, arugula and spinach salad.

ZUCCHINI & RAISIN PENNE

You could also serve this simple pasta dish with a scattering of crisp, golden bread crumbs (see page 80).

1 pound dried penne pasta • 2 tablespoons all-purpose flour • 2 zucchini, cut into matchsticks • 3 tablespoons olive oil • 2 garlic cloves, sliced • ½ teaspoon fennel seeds • 2 handfuls of pine nuts • 1 cup golden raisins • finely grated zest of 1 lemon • salt and freshly ground black pepper

TO SERVE: green salad

1 Bring a large saucepan of salted water to a boil and cook the penne until almost al dente, about 2 minutes less than directed on the package.
2 Meanwhile, season the flour with salt and pepper. Toss the zucchini matchsticks in the seasoned flour until lightly dusted.
3 Heat the olive oil in a large, deep, nonstick frying pan over medium heat. Fry the zucchini with the garlic and fennel seeds, stirring regularly, until light golden, 1 to 2 minutes.
4 Stir in the pine nuts and raisins and cook, stirring, until the pine nuts are golden and the raisins are softened, about 1 minute. Add the lemon zest and season to taste.
5 Using a slotted spoon, lift the pasta out of its cooking water and add to the frying pan. Cook, stirring, until the pasta is al dente, about 2 minutes. Serve with a green salad.

RICOTTA & FRESH HERB FRITTATA

This simple frittata, or flat omelet, is great for a swift dinner.

9 extra-large eggs, lightly beaten • ½ stick butter • 1 cup ricotta cheese • 1 small bunch of scallions, thinly sliced • 1 small bunch of chives, snipped • salt and freshly ground black pepper

TO SERVE: olive ciabatta bread, and tomato and lettuce salad

1 Preheat the broiler.
2 Season the eggs with salt and pepper. Melt the butter in a large, deep, nonstick frying pan with a heatproof handle. Pour in the eggs and cook over low heat until the base of the frittata is set and light golden, about 10 minutes.
3 Dollop small spoonfuls of the ricotta over the top, then place the frittata under the broiler, about 3 inches from the heat. Broil until the top is just set, 3 to 5 minutes. Scatter the scallions and chives over the frittata, then serve cut into wedges with slices of ciabatta and a lettuce and tomato salad.

ZUCCHINI & CANNELLINI BEAN SOUP

This is more like a thick purée than a soup, but it's gorgeous. It's finished with a drizzle of olive oil.

6 tablespoons extra-virgin olive oil • 1 small onion, chopped • 2 celery stalks, chopped • 2 garlic cloves, minced • 2 handfuls of parsley, leaves chopped • 2 pounds zucchini, roughly chopped • 14 ounces canned cannellini beans, drained and rinsed • salt and freshly ground black pepper

TO SERVE: crusty bread and blue cheese, such as Roquefort or Gorgonzola

1 Heat 2 tablespoons of the olive oil in a saucepan over medium heat. Fry the onion and celery with the garlic and half the parsley until softened but not colored, 4 to 5 minutes.
2 Add the zucchini and fry until softened and beginning to color, about 5 minutes.
3 Stir in ½ cup water and the cannellini beans. Cook 8 to 10 minutes, crushing the beans slightly with the back of a fork. Season with salt and plenty of pepper.
4 Ladle the soup into shallow soup bowls, drizzle the remaining olive oil over and sprinkle with the rest of the parsley. Serve with slices of crusty bread and a blue cheese of your choice.

CHERRY TOMATO CLAFOUTIS

This savory dish is based on the well-known sweet dessert, and makes a great dinner served with a fresh salad.

1 tablespoon butter • ¼ cup grated Parmesan cheese • 4 good handfuls of cherry tomatoes • 6 eggs, beaten • 1 cup heavy cream • ¾ cup all-purpose flour, sifted • 8 slices of ciabatta bread • extra-virgin olive oil, for drizzling • a few basil leaves • salt and freshly ground black pepper

TO SERVE: arugula, spinach and watercress salad

1 Preheat the oven to 400°F.
2 Grease four individual gratin dishes or 1 large dish with butter. Scatter 1 tablespoon of the Parmesan over the bottom of the dishes, then arrange the tomatoes evenly on top. Set aside.
3 Beat the eggs, cream and remaining Parmesan together until light and fluffy, then fold in the flour. Season with salt and pepper. Pour the mixture carefully over the tomatoes. Bake until risen and golden, 15 to 20 minutes.
4 Meanwhile, heat a ridged grill pan over high heat. Grill the ciabatta in two batches, turning once, until toasted and charred in places, 4 to 5 minutes. Drizzle a little olive oil over each slice.
5 Scatter the basil over the clafoutis and serve warm with the ciabatta and an arugula, spinach and watercress salad.

THIRTY MINUTES GIVES ENOUGH TIME TO PREPARE SOME SERIOUSLY BEAUTIFUL FOOD—AND YET IT ACTUALLY ISN'T A HUGE CHUNK OUT OF THE DAY. IT GOES TO PROVE THAT FAST FOOD CAN BE FABULOUS HOME-COOKED FOOD. TRY ONE FORKFUL OF SQUASH-BLOSSOM RISOTTO OR LAMB KEBABS WITH JEWELLED COUSCOUS AND I'M SURE YOU'LL AGREE.

THIRTY-MINUTE MEALS

STICKY CHICKEN WITH ALMOND COUSCOUS

You could substitute pieces of chicken breast or thigh meat for the wings, if preferred.

12 small chicken wings • juice of 1 orange • 1 tablespoon honey • 2 teaspoons mild curry paste • 1⅓ cups couscous • 2 cups hot vegetable or chicken stock • 1 large handful of toasted sliced almonds • 1 large handful of golden raisins • ¾ stick butter • 1 handful of parsley, leaves chopped • salt and freshly ground black pepper

TO SERVE: green salad with herbs

1 Preheat the oven to 400°F.
2 Arrange the chicken wings in a roasting pan and season with salt and pepper. Mix the orange juice, honey and curry paste together and spoon it over the chicken. Turn the chicken in the mixture until coated, then roast until cooked through and golden, about 25 minutes.
3 Meanwhile, put the couscous in a shallow baking dish and pour the hot stock over to cover. Stir, then cover and let stand until the stock is absorbed, 4 to 5 minutes. Fluff up the couscous with a fork and stir in the almonds and raisins. Season with salt and pepper. Dot half of the butter over the top and bake until heated through, about 10 minutes.
4 Remove the couscous from the oven and stir in the remaining butter and the parsley. Spoon into a serving dish and top with the chicken, pouring over any sticky juices left in the roasting pan. Serve with a salad of mixed greens and herbs.

PROSCIUTTO-WRAPPED CHICKEN BREASTS

These succulent chicken parcels encase tasty sun-dried tomatoes and aromatic sage.

4 skinless, boneless chicken breast halves, each about 6 ounces • 8 sun-dried tomatoes in oil, drained • 8 small sage leaves • 8 slices of prosciutto • 2 tablespoons olive oil • ⅓ cup dry white wine • 1 pound new potatoes • ¼ stick butter • 3 cups frozen peas • salt and freshly ground black pepper

1 Place a chicken breast between two sheets of plastic wrap and flatten with a meat mallet or rolling pin; repeat with the remaining chicken. Halve each breast and season with salt and pepper.
2 Place a sun-dried tomato and a small sage leaf toward the end of each piece of chicken. Roll up each piece three times, then wrap in a slice of prosciutto to make a parcel.
3 Heat the olive oil in a large, nonstick frying pan over medium heat. Fry the parcels until the prosciutto is golden and the chicken cooked through, about 10 minutes per side. Pour in the wine and season to taste. Cook, scraping any bits from the bottom of the pan, until the wine has reduced, about 3 minutes.
4 Meanwhile, cook the new potatoes in a saucepan of boiling salted water until tender, 15 to 20 minutes; drain and toss with half the butter.
5 Cook the peas in boiling water 3 to 4 minutes. Drain and toss with the remaining butter. Serve the chicken with the peas and new potatoes.

BAKED CHICKEN BREASTS IN TOMATO & MASCARPONE

A handful of black olives added to the creamy tomato sauce will add an extra depth of flavor, and a lovely contrast in color.

4 skinless, boneless chicken breast halves, each about 6 ounces • 3 shallots, chopped • 2 garlic cloves, sliced • 4 handfuls of cherry tomatoes, cut in half • 6 tablespoons dry white wine • 2 tablespoons olive oil • ¼ cup mascarpone cheese • 1 small handful of basil leaves • salt and freshly ground black pepper

TO SERVE: spinach salad and ciabatta bread

1 Preheat the oven to 400°F.
2 Arrange the chicken breasts in a baking dish and scatter the shallots and garlic over. Place the tomatoes on top of and around the chicken.
3 Pour in the white wine and drizzle the olive oil over the chicken. Season with salt and pepper. Bake 20 minutes.
4 Remove from the oven and dot the mascarpone randomly over and around the chicken. Return the dish to the oven and bake until the mascarpone just starts to melt in little puddles, about 5 minutes. Garnish with basil leaves and serve with slices of ciabatta and a spinach salad.

GOLDEN TURKEY CUTLETS WITH TARATOR

Tarator sauce is a specialty of Turkey, where it is often served with grilled fish or chicken. It's great with turkey cutlets, too. Try not to over-process the sauce—it shouldn't be too smooth.

3 tablespoons all-purpose flour • 1 tablespoon minced parsley leaves • 4 turkey breast cutlets, each about 6 ounces • 1 egg, beaten • 3 tablespoons olive oil • 2¾ pounds canned lima beans, drained and rinsed • 2 garlic cloves, minced • 4 tablespoons extra-virgin olive oil
TARATOR: 2 small slices of white bread • 2 garlic cloves, minced • heaped ½ cup walnut pieces • juice of ½ lemon, or to taste • ⅓ cup extra-virgin olive oil • salt and freshly ground black pepper

TO SERVE: green salad

1 To make the tarator sauce, put the bread in a food processor and blitz to crumbs. Add the garlic and walnuts, and blitz to a coarse paste. Add the lemon juice and olive oil and season with salt and pepper. Blitz briefly until combined, then set aside.
2 Mix the flour with the parsley and season to taste.
3 Dip the turkey in the egg and shake to remove any excess, then turn in the flour mixture to coat.
4 Heat the olive oil in a large, nonstick frying pan over medium heat. Fry the turkey until golden and cooked through, about 4 minutes per side.
5 While the turkey is cooking, heat the lima beans with the garlic and olive oil in a pan until warmed through, stirring occasionally. Using a hand blender, purée the beans, then season. Serve the turkey with the puréed lima beans, tarator and a salad of mixed greens.

HONEYED DUCK IN POMEGRANATE SAUCE

1 pound new potatoes • 1 tablespoon butter
• 4 duck breasts, each about 6 ounces
• 2 tablespoons honey • 3 tablespoons extra-virgin olive oil • 1 pound trimmed fine green beans
• seeds from 1 pomegranate
POMEGRANATE SAUCE: ½ cup olive oil
• 3 shallots, chopped • 2 garlic cloves, minced
• 1 handful of dried apricots, minced
• 2 tablespoons pomegranate molasses
• 1 tablespoon honey • 4 tablespoons Worcestershire sauce • ½ cup chicken stock
• salt and freshly ground black pepper

1 Preheat the oven to 400°F.
2 Cook the potatoes in boiling water until tender, 15 to 20 minutes; drain and toss with the butter.
3 Meanwhile, make the pomegranate sauce: Heat half the olive oil in a pan over medium heat and fry the shallots and garlic until softened, about 2 minutes. Add the apricots, molasses, honey and Worcestershire sauce. Stir in the stock and bring to a boil, then turn the heat down and simmer until reduced and thickened, 8 to 10 minutes; season.
4 Heat the remaining olive oil in a large, nonstick frying pan over medium heat. Fry the duck breasts, skin-side down, until the skin is golden, about 2 minutes. Turn them over and cook 2 minutes longer. Transfer the duck to a roasting pan and brush with honey. Season to taste and roast until cooked, about 12 minutes.
5 Cook the beans in boiling salted water until tender, 3 to 4 minutes; drain. To serve, slice the duck breasts and fan them out on plates. Spoon the sauce over, scatter the pomegranate seeds on top, and serve with green beans and new potatoes.

CRISP DUCK LASAGNE >

This isn't "lasagne" in the Italian sense, but crisp wonton skins filled with a vibrant duck salad.

peanut oil, for deep-frying • 8 wonton skins
• 1 garlic clove, minced • 1 tablespoon honey
• 1 tablespoon light soy sauce • 1 tablespoon tamarind paste • 1 teaspoon wholegrain mustard
• juice of 1 lime • 1 pound skinless duck breasts, cut into strips • 1 large carrot, cut into ribbons
• 4 scallions, diagonally sliced • 1 small red bell pepper, seeded and sliced • 1 handful of sugar snap peas • 1 handful of bean sprouts • 2 handfuls of herb salad, including cilantro • 2 teaspoons toasted sesame seeds • salt and freshly ground black pepper
DRESSING: 4 tablespoons peanut oil • 4 pieces preserved ginger in syrup, chopped, plus 4 tablespoons syrup • 2 tablespoons soy sauce

1 Preheat the broiler.
2 Heat the oil in a wok and deep-fry the wontons, in two batches, until golden, which will only take a few seconds. Drain on paper towels and set aside.
3 In a large bowl, mix together the garlic, honey, soy sauce, tamarind, mustard and lime juice. Toss the duck strips in the mixture to coat. Broil the duck, about 4 inches from the heat, until glossy and cooked, 8 to 10 minutes; during cooking, turn once and baste with the marinade.
4 Meanwhile, put all the vegetables and herb salad in a bowl. Mix together the ingredients for the dressing and season with salt and pepper, then spoon enough over the salad to coat it lightly.
5 Lay a wonton skin on each serving plate. Top with a handful of the salad and then the duck. Place a second wonton skin on the duck. Drizzle any remaining salad dressing over, sprinkle with the sesame seeds and serve.

< PORK BURGERS WITH BLUE CHEESE & RED ONION SALSA

These succulent burgers are best made with a punchy blue cheese.

1 pound ground pork • 1 onion, minced • 2 tablespoons soy sauce • 4 ounces blue cheese, such as Roquefort, Gorgonzola or Stilton, sliced • salt and freshly ground black pepper
RED ONION SALSA: 2 tablespoons olive oil • 2 red onions, cut into thin wedges • 2 tablespoons balsamic vinegar • 1 tablespoon chili oil

TO SERVE: 4 crusty burger buns and arugula salad

1 Preheat the broiler.
2 In a large bowl, mix together the pork, onion and soy sauce, and season with salt and pepper. Form the mixture into four patties.
3 Broil the burgers, about 4 inches from the heat, until well browned and cooked through, about 4 minutes per side. Top each burger with one-fourth of the cheese and broil until melted.
4 While the burgers are cooking, make the red onion salsa. Heat 1 tablespoon of the olive oil in a ridged grill pan over high heat. Grill the onion wedges, turning occasionally, until softened and charred in places, about 10 minutes. Remove from the heat and stir in the balsamic vinegar, chili oil and the remaining olive oil.
5 Place one half of a bun on each serving plate. Top with a burger and a spoonful of the onion salsa. Place the other half of the buns on top and serve with an arugula salad.

PORK IN MUSHROOM & MUSTARD SAUCE

This dish of pork chops in a creamy mushroom sauce is served with puréed white beans and zucchini—ideal for a special occasion.

2 tablespoons olive oil • 4 garlic cloves (2 sliced and 2 minced) • 4 thick pork chops, each about 6 ounces • 1 pound cremini mushrooms, sliced • 6 tablespoons Marsala • 4 tablespoons heavy cream • 1 tablespoon wholegrain mustard • 1 handful of parsley, leaves chopped • 1¼ pounds zucchini, sliced • 6 tablespoons extra-virgin olive oil • 2¾ pounds canned cannellini beans, drained and rinsed • salt and freshly ground black pepper

1 Heat the olive oil in a large, nonstick frying pan over medium heat and fry the sliced garlic 30 seconds. Add the chops and cook, turning once, until golden, 7 to 8 minutes. Add the mushrooms and cook, stirring often, 5 minutes longer.
2 Add the Marsala and bubble 3 to 4 minutes, then stir in the cream, mustard and parsley. Season with salt and pepper. Simmer gently until the sauce has thickened and the chops are cooked through, about 3 minutes.
3 While the pork is cooking, heat 3 tablespoons of the extra-virgin olive oil in a large, nonstick frying pan over medium-high heat. Fry the zucchini until softened and golden, 3 to 4 minutes.
4 Put the beans in a pan with the remaining extra-virgin olive oil and the minced garlic. Heat until warmed through, stirring occasionally. Using a hand blender, purée the beans, then season. Serve the pork with the bean purée and zucchini.

CANNELLINI BEAN & SAUSAGE STEW

Use meaty fresh sausages and the results will be delicious. For fans of all things fiery, a crumbled dried chili adds extra "oomph", but you can leave it out, if preferred.

2 tablespoons olive oil • 1 onion, sliced • 8 fresh pork link sausages • 14 ounces canned cherry tomatoes • 1 cup beef or chicken stock • 1 teaspoon fennel seeds • 1 dried chili (mildly hot or hot, to taste; optional) • 14 ounces canned cannellini beans, drained and rinsed • 4 cups baby spinach leaves • 1 handful of parsley, leaves chopped • salt and freshly ground black pepper

1 Heat the olive oil in a large, deep sauté pan over medium heat. Fry the onion and sausages, stirring often, until the sausages are golden all over, about 5 minutes.
2 Add the tomatoes, stock and fennel seeds, then crumble in the chili, if using. Add the cannellini beans and season with salt and pepper.
3 Bring to a boil, then turn the heat down and simmer 15 minutes. Stir in the spinach and continue simmering until the sausages are cooked and the sauce has reduced and thickened, about 5 minutes. Stir in the parsley and serve.

HAM WITH LENTILS & POACHED EGGS

Vincotto is a lovely, rich specialty vinegar from Italy. Its deep, sweet flavor marries beautifully with the earthiness of lentils. Add salty ham and a runny egg and you have a heavenly dish.

1½ cups Puy lentils • 4 ham steaks, each about 6 ounces • 5 tablespoons extra-virgin olive oil • a splash of white wine vinegar • 4 extra-large eggs • 1 onion, chopped • 1 garlic clove, minced • 2 tablespoons vincotto (or balsamic vinegar) • salt and freshly ground black pepper

TO SERVE: arugula salad

1 Cook the lentils in boiling water until tender, about 20 minutes.
2 Meanwhile, preheat the broiler. Brush the ham steaks with 1 tablespoon of the oil, then broil, 4 to 5 inches from the heat, until cooked, 2 to 3 minutes per side.
3 Bring a large frying pan of water to a boil and add the wine vinegar. Turn the heat down to low. Break the eggs, one at a time, onto a saucer, then slide them into the water. Quickly gather the whites neatly around the yolk using a spoon and poach until cooked, about 3 minutes.
4 While the eggs are poaching, heat 2 tablespoons of the olive oil in a large, nonstick frying pan over medium heat. Fry the onion and garlic until softened, about 2 minutes. Drain the lentils and add them to the onions, then stir in the vincotto and the remaining olive oil. Season to taste.
5 Serve the lentils with the egg, ham steaks and an arugula salad.

LAMB KEBABS WITH JEWELLED COUSCOUS

These lamb kebabs are inspired by a dish known as *arrosticini*, which is a specialty of the Abruzzo region in Italy. In Abruzzo, it is made with mutton, but lamb is just as delicious. You will need 4 metal skewers.

1 pound lean boneless lamb, diced • 1⅓ cups couscous • 2 cups hot vegetable or chicken stock • seeds from 1 pomegranate • 1 large handful of shelled unsalted pistachio nuts • ¼ cup frozen corn kernels, thawed • 1 handful of dried cranberries or sour cherries • ¾ stick butter • 1 handful of cilantro, chopped • salt and freshly ground black pepper

TO SERVE: watercress salad

1 Preheat the oven to 400°F.
2 Thread six pieces of lamb onto each skewer.
3 Put the couscous in a shallow baking dish and pour the hot stock over to cover. Stir, then cover and let stand until the stock is absorbed, 4 to 5 minutes. Fluff up the couscous with a fork, then stir in the pomegranate seeds, pistachios, corn and cranberries.
4 Dot half of the butter evenly over the top and place in the oven to heat through 10 minutes. Remove from the oven and stir in the remaining butter and the cilantro. Keep warm.
5 Preheat the broiler. Season the lamb with salt and pepper, then broil, 3 to 4 inches from the heat, turning often, until cooked through, about 5 minutes. Serve the lamb kebabs with the couscous and a watercress salad.

SEARED LAMB WITH CINNAMON ONIONS

Don't be tempted to add more cinnamon—you just want to give a pleasant hint of spice, rather than it being overwhelming.

1 pound lean boneless lamb, sliced • 2 tablespoons olive oil • 1 teaspoon thyme leaves • 14 ounces canned chickpeas, drained and rinsed • 2 garlic cloves, minced • 3 tablespoons extra-virgin olive oil • salt and freshly ground black pepper
CINNAMON ONIONS: 2 tablespoons olive oil • 3 red onions, thinly sliced • 1 teaspoon ground cinnamon • 1 tablespoon sugar • ½ cup red wine • 2 tablespoons red wine vinegar

TO SERVE: spinach salad

1 To make the cinnamon onions, heat the oil in a large, nonstick frying pan over medium heat and fry the onions with the cinnamon 1 minute, stirring frequently. Add the sugar and cook 1 minute longer. Pour in the red wine, wine vinegar and 3 tablespoons water. Bring to a boil, then turn the heat down and simmer, stirring regularly, until the onions are soft and sticky, about 20 minutes.
2 Meanwhile, brush the lamb with the olive oil and season with salt and pepper, then sprinkle with the thyme. Heat a ridged grill pan over medium-high heat and sear the lamb until cooked to your liking, about 2 minutes per side for medium-rare.
3 Put the chickpeas in a pan with 3 tablespoons hot water, the garlic and extra-virgin olive oil. Heat, stirring occasionally. Using a hand blender, purée the beans, then season. Serve the lamb with the bean purée, cinnamon onions and a spinach salad.

STEAK IN MARSALA

Marsala is a Sicilian fortified wine that adds a wonderful flavor to both savory and sweet sauces. You don't have to pay a fortune for a bottle, and a little goes a long way, so it's well worth keeping some on hand.

1¼ pounds boiling potatoes, peeled and cut into chunks • 3 tablespoons hot milk • 4 tablespoons olive oil • 2 onions, very thinly sliced • 4 boneless sirloin steaks, each about 6 ounces • ¾ cup Marsala • 1 pound broccoli florets • salt and freshly ground black pepper

1 Cook the potatoes in boiling salted water until soft, 15 to 20 minutes; drain well. Add the hot milk and 1 tablespoon of the olive oil and mash until smooth. Keep warm.
2 While the potatoes are cooking, heat half the olive oil in a large, nonstick frying pan over medium heat. Fry the onions, stirring regularly, until softened and golden in places, about 10 minutes.
3 Heat a ridged grill pan over high heat. Brush the steaks with the remaining oil and season with salt and pepper, then grill until cooked to your liking, 2 to 3 minutes per side for medium-rare.
4 Add the onions to the pan with the steaks and stir in the Marsala. Bubble until the Marsala has reduced and thickened and the onions are glossy, 2 to 3 minutes.
5 Meanwhile, cook the broccoli in boiling salted water until tender, 4 to 5 minutes; drain. Serve the steaks with the sauce spooned over and with the mashed potatoes and broccoli.

ROASTED MEATBALLS IN LEMON & BAY >

These tasty meatballs are simply roasted in white wine with thin wedges of lemon and fragrant bay leaves. Ground pork can be used instead of veal, if preferred.

1 pound ground veal • 1 cup grated Parmesan cheese • 1 teaspoon dried oregano • 6 sage leaves, minced • 2 tablespoons olive oil • ⅔ cup dry white wine • 1 lemon, cut into thin wedges • 6 bay leaves • 1 pound dried spaghetti • salt and freshly ground black pepper

TO SERVE: green salad

1 Preheat the oven to 425°F.
2 Put the veal into a bowl and mix in the Parmesan and herbs. Season with salt and pepper. Form into walnut-size balls.
3 Heat the olive oil in a large, nonstick frying pan over high heat. Fry the meatballs, turning occasionally, until lightly browned, 3 to 4 minutes.
4 Transfer the meatballs to a baking dish and pour in the wine. Scatter the lemon wedges and bay leaves over the top, then bake until the meatballs are cooked through, about 20 minutes.
5 Meanwhile, cook the spaghetti: Bring a large pan of salted water to a boil and cook the spaghetti until al dente, about 10 minutes. Drain and toss with the meatballs and any juices. Transfer to a serving dish and serve with a salad of mixed greens.

< SMOKED HADDOCK GRATIN

Instead of potatoes, crusty bread would also be good with this creamy fish gratin.

1 pound baby new potatoes • ½ stick butter • 2¼ pounds smoked haddock fillet (finnan haddie) • 1 bay leaf • 1¼ cups milk • 2 tablespoons all-purpose flour • ⅔ cup heavy cream • 2 teaspoons wholegrain mustard • 2 egg yolks • ¼ cup grated Parmesan cheese • 2¼ pounds spinach leaves, washed • freshly ground black pepper

1 Preheat the oven to 400°F.
2 Cook the new potatoes in boiling salted water until tender, about 15 minutes. Drain and toss with 1 tablespoon of the butter; keep hot.
3 While the potatoes are cooking, put the haddock in a large frying pan, add the bay leaf and pour in the milk. Cook over medium-low heat until the fish is just opaque, about 5 minutes. Remove from the pan. Check for any bones, then remove the skin and flake the flesh. Place in a baking dish. Strain the milk and reserve.
4 Melt 2 tablespoons of the butter in a saucepan over medium heat. Add the flour and cook, stirring, 3 minutes. Gradually pour in the poaching milk and cook, stirring, until thickened, about 2 minutes. Whisk in the cream, mustard and egg yolks, then season with pepper. Stir in half the Parmesan. Spoon the sauce over the fish. Sprinkle the remaining Parmesan over the top and bake until golden, about 10 minutes.
5 Meanwhile, steam the spinach, 2 minutes. Drain well, then toss with the remaining butter. Serve the gratin with the new potatoes and spinach.

MINI SALMON EN CROÛTES

Individual phyllo parcels filled with salmon, ginger and currants are served with a creamy watercress sauce. Bliss!

1 pound skinless salmon fillet, cut into ½-inch cubes • 1 teaspoon lemon juice • 3 pieces preserved ginger in syrup, minced • 2 tablespoons currants • ¾ stick butter, melted • 1 tablespoon chopped cilantro • 8 (8-inch) squares phyllo pastry • 1¼ cups light cream • 1 large handful of watercress • 1 tablespoon wholegrain mustard • 28 ounces canned flageolet or small lima beans, drained and rinsed • 2 tablespoons extra-virgin olive oil • 1 small handful of chopped parsley • salt and freshly ground black pepper

1 Preheat the oven to 400°F.
2 Put the salmon in a bowl. Stir in the lemon juice, ginger, currants, cilantro and 4 tablespoons of the melted butter. Season with salt and pepper.
3 Lay one of the phyllo squares on the worktop and brush lightly with some of the remaining melted butter. Top with a second square. Put one-fourth of the salmon mixture in the center and fold over the edges to enclose the filling and create a square parcel. Repeat to make three more parcels.
4 Transfer the parcels to a nonstick baking sheet, seam-side down, and brush with butter. Bake until the pastry is golden, about 10 minutes.
5 Meanwhile, purée the cream and watercress in a food processor. Add the mustard and seasoning.
6 Put the beans in a pan with the olive oil. Heat, stirring occasionally, then add the parsley. Serve the parcels with the beans and watercress sauce.

CRAB & CORN CAKES WITH MANGO SALSA

The mango salsa here is one of those recipes that you can play around with to suit your own palate and what's available. For example, you could add a little fresh chili (mildly hot or hot, to taste).

heaped 1 cup frozen corn kernels, thawed • 1 tablespoon all-purpose flour • 1 egg, beaten • 2 cups crabmeat • 1 small handful of parsley, leaves chopped • 3 to 4 tablespoons olive oil • sunflower oil, for deep frying • 12 wonton skins **MANGO SALSA:** 1 small red onion, minced • 2 bell peppers (1 red and 1 yellow), seeded and diced • 1 ripe but firm mango, pitted and diced • 1 ripe but firm avocado, pitted and diced • 4 tomatoes, seeded and diced • finely grated zest and juice of 2 limes • 1 large handful of cilantro, leaves chopped • salt and freshly ground black pepper

1 To make the salsa, mix together all the ingredients in a bowl. Season with salt and pepper; set aside.
2 To make the crab cakes, put the corn, flour and egg in a bowl and stir until well mixed. Lightly fold in the crabmeat and parsley, then season.
3 Heat the olive oil in a large, nonstick frying pan over medium heat. Place four generous tablespoons of the batter in the pan, leaving a little space between each one, and fry until golden, 2 to 3 minutes per side. Drain on paper towels and keep warm while frying more fritters, to make 12 fritters in total.
4 Heat enough sunflower oil in a wok or large pan to deep-fry the wontons. When the oil is very hot, fry the skins until golden and puffed up, about 30 seconds, then drain on paper towels. Serve hot with the fritters and salsa.

ROASTED SEA BASS WITH STOVED POTATOES >

This works best with fillets cut from a large fish, but if you find that only small fish are available, allow two per person and use an extra roasting pan.

6 tablespoons olive oil • 1½ pounds waxy potatoes, peeled and cut into bite-size pieces • 4 large garlic cloves, unpeeled • 4 large sea bass fillets • 2 lemons, cut into wedges • 3 handfuls of snow peas • salt and freshly ground black pepper

1 Heat 4 tablespoons of the olive oil in a large, nonstick sauté pan over high heat. Add the potatoes and garlic and stir to coat them in the oil, then turn down the heat to medium-low and cover with a lid. Cook until soft and golden, about 20 minutes, giving the pan a shake from time to time to prevent sticking. Drain the potatoes briefly on paper towels and season with salt; keep warm.
2 Meanwhile, preheat the oven to 400°F.
3 Lay the fish fillets in a roasting pan. Pour the remaining olive oil over the top, squeeze half of the lemon wedges over the fish and top with the remaining wedges. Season to taste, then roast until cooked, about 10 minutes.
4 Steam the snow peas until tender, 3 to 4 minutes. Serve the fish with the stoved potatoes and garlic and the snow peas.

< FISH TAGINE

Choose a selection of seafood, including fish, baby squid (calamari), shrimp, mussels and clams. Mussels are essential because of the gorgeous juices they release into the broth.

6 tablespoons extra-virgin olive oil • 1 red bell pepper, seeded and minced • pinch of saffron threads • ¾-inch piece fresh ginger root, peeled and grated • 1¼ pounds very ripe tomatoes, seeded and diced • ⅔ cup dry white wine • 3½ pounds assorted raw shellfish and fish, cleaned and scaled as needed • 1 small handful of parsley, leaves chopped • 1⅔ cups couscous • 2 cups hot vegetable stock • ¼ stick butter • salt and freshly ground black pepper

TO SERVE: crusty bread and green salad

1 Heat the olive oil in a large, deep sauté pan over low heat. Add the bell pepper, saffron, ginger and tomatoes and cook gently, stirring occasionally, until the pepper and tomatoes are meltingly soft, about 10 minutes.
2 Pour in the wine and season with salt and pepper, then add the shellfish and any large fish. Cover with a lid and cook 2 minutes.
3 Add the squid, if using, and any smaller fish at this point. Continue to simmer until the fish is just cooked, about 5 minutes.
4 Meanwhile, put the couscous in a bowl and pour the hot stock over to cover. Stir, then cover and let stand until the stock is absorbed, 5 to 6 minutes. Fluff up with a fork and stir in the butter.
5 Scatter the parsley over the tagine and serve with the couscous, bread for mopping up the juices, and a green salad.

TUNA CAKES WITH TOMATO-CAPER SAUCE

The tomato-caper sauce is a perfect accompaniment for these simple fishcakes, but they're also fantastic with bottled ketchup!

1 pound 2 ounces jarred or canned tuna in olive oil • 2 thick slices of white bread, crusts removed • 1 egg, lightly beaten • 1 heaped cup grated sharp Cheddar cheese • 4 tablespoons olive oil • 2 cups frozen peas • salt and freshly ground black pepper
TOMATO-CAPER SAUCE: 3 tablespoons olive oil • 1 onion, minced • 2 garlic cloves, minced • 14 ounces canned cherry tomatoes • 2 teaspoons sugar • 1 tablespoon capers, drained and rinsed • 1 small handful of basil leaves, roughly torn

1 To make the sauce, heat the olive oil in a pan over low heat and fry the onion and garlic until softened, about 5 minutes. Add the cherry tomatoes and sugar, and season with salt and pepper. Bring to a boil, then turn the heat down and simmer until reduced and thickened, 10 to 15 minutes. Add the capers and basil, then simmer 5 minutes longer.
2 Meanwhile, put the tuna and its oil in a large bowl and flake with a fork. Blitz the bread in a food processor to make crumbs, and add to the tuna. Stir in the egg and cheese and season with salt and pepper. Form into eight patties.
3 Heat the olive oil in a large, nonstick frying pan over medium heat. Fry the tuna cakes, turning once, until golden, about 4 to 5 minutes. Drain on paper towels.
4 Cook the peas in boiling water 3 to 4 minutes; drain. Serve the tuna cakes with the tomato-caper sauce and peas.

CRISP BEAN CAKES WITH CHILI-LIME DIP

This recipe makes the sort of quick and easy dinner that both vegetarians and meat-eaters will enjoy.

28 ounces canned large lima beans, drained and rinsed • 2 garlic cloves, minced • ⅓ cup grated Parmesan cheese • 3 tablespoons ketchup • 1¼ cups fresh bread crumbs • 3 tablespoons olive oil • salt and freshly ground black pepper
CHILI-LIME DIP: 6 tablespoons chili sauce • juice of 1 lime

TO SERVE: crusty bread and green salad

1 To make the dip, mix the chili sauce and lime juice together in a small bowl; set aside.
2 Put the lima beans in a large bowl with the garlic, Parmesan, ketchup and bread crumbs. Using a hand blender, blend until coarse-fine, or mash with a fork if you prefer the bean cakes to have a slightly coarser texture. Season with salt and pepper. Form into small patties about 1¼ inches in diameter.
3 Heat the olive oil in a large, nonstick frying pan over medium heat. Fry the bean cakes until golden and crisp, 2 to 3 minutes per side (you will need to cook them in two batches). Drain on paper towels and keep warm.
4 Serve the bean cakes with the chili-lime dip, slices of crusty bread and a green salad.

CREAMED MUSHROOMS WITH POLENTA

Any firm, meaty mushrooms will work well in this recipe. It's also good made with fresh wild mushrooms when they're in season.

3 tablespoons olive oil • 4 shallots, minced • 2 garlic cloves, minced • 2¼ pounds small cremini mushrooms • ½ cup Marsala • 1 cup heavy cream • 2 tablespoons wholegrain mustard • 1 small handful of tarragon, leaves minced • 1 pound broccolini • salt and freshly ground black pepper
POLENTA: 4 cups vegetable stock • 1⅔ cups instant polenta • 1 cup grated Parmesan cheese • 2 teaspoons coarsely cracked black peppercorns • ¼ stick butter, softened

1 To make the polenta, bring the stock to a rolling boil in a pan. Add the polenta in a steady stream, stirring with a large balloon whisk. Bring back to a boil, then turn the heat down and simmer until thickened, 6 to 8 minutes.
2 Using a wooden spoon, stir in the Parmesan, pepper and butter. Taste. season with salt, if necessary, and keep warm.
3 Heat the olive oil in a large saucepan over medium heat and fry the shallots and garlic until softened, about 2 minutes. Add the mushrooms and cook 2 minutes longer, stirring often. Pour in the Marsala and bubble briefly until reduced. Turn the heat down a little, then stir in the cream, mustard and tarragon. Warm through, then season to taste.
4 Meanwhile, steam the broccoli until just tender, about 5 minutes. Serve the mushrooms on top of the polenta with the broccoli alongside.

TOMATO TARTE TATIN

For this summery tart, it's important that the oven is very hot to ensure the pastry is thoroughly cooked, puffed up and golden. Before serving, you could scatter a few toasted pine nuts over the tart, if liked.

1 pound new potatoes • 1 tablespoon butter • 1¼ pounds cherry tomatoes • 3 tablespoons olive oil • ½ teaspoon sugar • 1 tablespoon thyme leaves • 1 sheet puff pastry, about 9 ounces, thawed if frozen • salt and freshly ground black pepper

TO SERVE: arugula and shaved Parmesan salad

1 Preheat the oven to 425°F.
2 Cook the potatoes in boiling salted water until soft, 15 to 20 minutes. Drain and toss with the butter.
3 Meanwhile, arrange the tomatoes, cut-side up, over the bottom of an 8-inch tarte tatin pan or round cake pan that is about 1½ inches deep. Drizzle the olive oil over the tomatoes. Sprinkle with the sugar and thyme, and season with salt and pepper. Bake until starting to soften, about 5 minutes.
4 Trim the pastry to fit the pan, with a ¾-inch overhang. Lay the pastry carefully over the tomatoes and tuck the overhang down inside the sides of the pan. Bake until the pastry is risen and golden, about 15 minutes.
5 Remove the tart from the oven and carefully unmold it, pastry-side down, onto a plate. Serve warm with the new potatoes and an arugula and shaved Parmesan salad.

TOMATO, RICOTTA & SPINACH STRUDEL

The classic combination of ricotta and spinach is wonderful enclosed in crisp, light phyllo pastry.

2 tablespoons olive oil • 1 garlic clove, minced • 1 large onion, chopped • 1 pound tomatoes, cut in half and seeded • 1 pound baby spinach leaves, washed • heaped 1 cup ricotta cheese • 4 sheets of phyllo pastry, each about 10 x 12 inches • ⅓ stick butter, melted • salt and freshly ground black pepper

TO SERVE: watercress salad

1 Preheat the oven to 425°F.
2 Heat the olive oil in a large saucepan over medium heat and fry the garlic and onion until soft, about 3 minutes. Add the tomatoes and cook until they are beginning to break down, about 3 minutes.
3 Put the spinach in a separate pan with only the water left clinging to the leaves after washing. Cook over low heat until wilted, about 2 minutes. Drain, squeezing out any excess moisture, then chop. Stir the spinach into the tomato mixture and add the ricotta. Season with salt and pepper and mix well.
4 Lay one sheet of phyllo on the worktop and brush with a little of the melted butter. Top with a second sheet of phyllo and brush with more butter. Repeat with the remaining phyllo, brushing each layer with butter. Spoon the spinach filling along the center, then fold in the ends and the sides of the phyllo to form a rectangular-shaped parcel.
5 Carefully lift the parcel onto a nonstick baking sheet, seam-side down. Brush the remaining butter all over the parcel. Bake until crisp and golden, about 15 minutes. Serve with a watercress salad.

PEA, ROSEMARY & MASCARPONE RISOTTO

Creamy risotto flecked with peas, rosemary and pools of mascarpone makes a totally irresistible dish. For non-vegetarians, some crisp pancetta crumbled over the top just before serving adds a nice touch.

3 tablespoons olive oil • 1 onion, minced • 1 tablespoon minced rosemary • 1⅓ cups risotto rice • 1¼ cups dry white wine • 3 cups hot vegetable stock • ½ cup grated Parmesan cheese • 1½ cups frozen peas • ⅓ cup mascarpone cheese • salt and freshly ground black pepper

TO SERVE: spinach, arugula and watercress salad

1 Heat the olive oil in a large, deep sauté pan over low heat and fry the onion with the rosemary until softened, but not colored, 2 to 3 minutes. Add the rice and stir until it is coated in the oil and glossy, 2 to 3 minutes. Stir in the wine and bubble 30 seconds.
2 Keep the vegetable stock hot in a saucepan over low heat. Add a ladleful of hot stock to the rice and cook over medium-low heat, stirring constantly, until it has been absorbed, 2 to 3 minutes. Continue adding the stock, a little at a time. When all the stock has been absorbed, the rice will be soft, but still have a little resistance. Total cooking time will be 20 to 25 minutes. About 5 minutes before the rice is ready, stir in the peas.
3 Add the Parmesan, then season with salt and pepper. Lightly fold in the mascarpone. Serve with a spinach, watercress and arugula salad.

SQUASH-BLOSSOM RISOTTO >

It's such a pity that squash blossoms make such a fleeting appearance in markets because they're gorgeous fried in a crisp light batter, or stirred into a creamy risotto like this one. Take care with the saffron, since too much will mask the delicate flavor of the flowers.

3 tablespoons olive oil • 1 onion, minced • a pinch of saffron threads • 1⅓ cups risotto rice • 1¼ cups dry white wine • 3 cups hot vegetable stock • ½ cup grated Parmesan cheese • ⅓ cup mascarpone cheese • 2 handfuls of squash blossoms • salt and freshly ground black pepper

TO SERVE: zucchini, herb and squash-blossom salad

1 Heat the olive oil in a large, deep sauté pan over low heat and fry the onion with the saffron until softened, but not colored, 2 to 3 minutes. Add the rice and stir until it is coated in the oil and glossy, 2 to 3 minutes. Stir in the wine and bubble for 30 seconds.
2 Keep the vegetable stock hot in a saucepan over low heat. Add a ladleful of hot stock to the rice and cook over medium-low heat, stirring constantly, until it has been absorbed, 2 to 3 minutes. Continue adding the stock, a little at a time. When all the stock has been absorbed, the rice will be soft, but still have a little resistance. Total cooking time will be 20 to 25 minutes.
3 Stir in the Parmesan, then season with salt and pepper. Lightly fold in the squash blossoms and the mascarpone. Serve with a salad of zucchini, herbs and squash blossoms.

VEGETABLE CURRY WITH COCONUT RICE

Poppadoms and mango chutney can also be served alongside the curry and basmati rice.

2 tablespoons olive oil • 1 onion, chopped • 2 garlic cloves, chopped • 1 tbsp curry paste • 2 carrots, chopped • 2 parsnips, chopped • 2 potatoes, peeled and cut into bite-size chunks • 2 zucchini, chopped • 1 handful of small cauliflower florets • 1¼ cups vegetable stock • 1¼ cups basmati rice • 1¾ cups canned coconut milk • 1 handful of golden raisins • 2 tablespoons mango chutney • 1 handful of toasted sliced almonds • salt and freshly ground black pepper

1 Heat the olive oil in a large saucepan over medium heat and fry the onion and garlic 2 minutes. Stir in the curry paste. Add the vegetables and pour in the stock. Bring to a boil, then turn the heat down, cover and simmer until the vegetables are tender, 15 to 20 minutes.
2 Meanwhile, put the rice in a medium-size saucepan with the coconut milk and 1 cup water. Bring to a boil, then turn the heat down, cover and simmer until the rice is cooked and the liquid is absorbed, about 15 minutes. Remove from the heat and let stand, covered, until ready to serve.
3 Drain the vegetables, saving the stock. Return two-thirds of the vegetables to the pan. Using a hand blender, purée the remaining vegetables, adding enough of the stock to make a sauce.
4 Gently stir the vegetable purée, raisins and mango chutney into the curry. Season with salt and pepper, then reheat gently.
5 Serve the curry with the almonds scattered over and the coconut rice.

CURRIED PARSNIP SOUP

Hand blenders are fabulous tools for puréeing soups and, of course, they are much easier to clean than a food processor or large blender. Adjust the amount of curry paste in this soup to suit your palate.

4 tablespoons olive oil • 1 onion, chopped • 2 teaspoons mild curry paste, or to taste • 1½ pounds parsnips, cut into chunks • 5 cups vegetable stock • 14 ounces canned chickpeas, drained and rinsed • ⅔ cup heavy cream • 1 handful of parsley, chopped • salt and freshly ground black pepper

TO SERVE: crusty bread and goat cheese

1 Heat 3 tablespoons of the olive oil in a large saucepan over medium heat and fry the onion until softened, 2 to 3 minutes. Stir in the curry paste, then add the parsnips. Cook 2 to 3 minutes longer.
2 Pour in the stock. Bring to a boil, then turn the heat down and simmer until the parsnips are tender, about 20 minutes.
3 Meanwhile, heat the remaining olive oil in a large, nonstick frying pan over medium heat. Fry the chickpeas, tossing them occasionally, until golden and slightly crisp, 8 to 10 minutes. Set aside until ready to serve.
4 Using a hand blender, purée the soup until smooth. Stir in the cream and parsley, and season with salt and pepper. Reheat gently. To serve, scatter the chickpeas over each bowl of soup and accompany with slices of crusty bread and goat cheese.

SPICY RED LENTILS

Coconut cream adds a really rich creaminess to this simple lentil dish. You can also use dried coconut milk powder, but make it up slightly thicker than suggested on the package—it should be the same consistency as coconut cream.

1 tablespoon cumin seeds • 1 tablespoon cilantro seeds • 2 teaspoons ground ginger • 2 tablespoons olive oil • 1 onion, chopped • 2 carrots, chopped • 1 small sweet potato, peeled and chopped • 2 cups dried red lentils • 14 ounces canned cherry tomatoes, drained • 3¾ cups vegetable stock • 1 teaspoon dark brown sugar • ⅓ cup canned coconut cream • 1 handful of parsley, leaves chopped • salt and freshly ground black pepper

TO SERVE: naan breads

1 Put the spices in a large saucepan and toast over medium heat, stirring, until they smell fragrant, 1 to 2 minutes.
2 Pour in the olive oil and add the onion. Fry, stirring, until slightly softened, about 2 minutes, then add the carrots, sweet potato, red lentils and cherry tomatoes.
3 Pour in the stock, add the sugar and season with salt and pepper. Bring to a boil, then turn the heat down and simmer until the vegetables and lentils are tender, about 20 minutes.
4 Stir in the coconut cream and parsley and cook 1 minute longer. Serve with naan breads.

POTATO, CHARD & GREEN BEAN BRAISE

Deliciously simple, this makes a great main dish. Non-vegetarians could top it with a few slices of crisp bacon, although it tastes very good as it is.

5 tablespoons olive oil • 1 garlic clove, sliced • 1 onion, chopped • 1¾ pounds potatoes, peeled and diced • 1¼ pounds trimmed green beans, cut into 1-inch pieces • 2¼ pounds Swiss chard, trimmed and chopped • 8 slices of olive ciabatta bread • 6 ounces soft goat cheese • salt and freshly ground black pepper

1 Heat 3 tablespoons of the olive oil in a large, deep, nonstick sauté pan over medium heat. Fry the garlic and onion 1 minute, then add the potatoes, green beans, chard and ½ cup water. Season with salt and pepper.
2 Cover with a lid and cook over medium-low heat until the vegetables are soft and all the water is absorbed, about 20 minutes.
3 Meanwhile, preheat the grill to high. Grill the olive ciabatta slices until toasted. Drizzle the remaining olive oil over them and top each slice with a spoonful of goat cheese. Season with pepper. Serve the cheese toasts with the vegetables.

ARTICHOKE, PINE NUT & PARMESAN TART

Puff pastry makes a great tart case but takes an age to make from scratch. Luckily chilled and frozen puff pastry is widely available now, so it seems silly not to make use of it.

1 pound baby new potatoes • ¼ stick butter • 1 sheet puff pastry, about 9 ounces, thawed if frozen • 11 ounces jarred, marinated artichoke hearts, drained well • 1 cup mascarpone cheese • 4 eggs • 1½ cups grated Parmesan cheese • 1 tablespoon toasted pine nuts • salt and freshly ground black pepper

TO SERVE: green salad

1 Preheat the oven to 425°F.
2 Put the potatoes in a saucepan and add enough water to half cover them. Season with a little salt, add the butter and cover with a lid. Cook over medium heat until tender, 20 to 25 minutes, stirring occasionally to prevent the potatoes from sticking.
3 Meanwhile, line a 9-inch nonstick tart pan with the puff pastry. Arrange the artichokes evenly over the bottom of the pastry shell.
4 Beat the mascarpone and eggs together until smooth. Stir in the Parmesan and season with salt and pepper. Pour the mixture into the tart case and scatter the pine nuts over the top. Bake until puffed up and golden, about 20 minutes.
5 Serve the tart with the potatoes and a salad of mixed greens.

EGGPLANT, MOZZARELLA & TOMATO BAKE >

This is also delicious made with silken tofu instead of mozzarella, making it a great dish for vegans or those with a dairy allergy.

2 small eggplants, each cut into 8 long slices • 6 tablespoons olive oil • 8 tomatoes, seeded and chopped • 1 dried chili (mildly hot or hot, to taste), crumbled • 9 ounces mozzarella cheese, diced • 1 cup roughly chopped walnuts • 1 small handful of parsley, leaves chopped • salt and freshly ground black pepper

TO SERVE: ciabatta bread and watercress salad

1 Preheat the oven to 400°F.
2 Heat a ridged grill pan over high heat. Brush the eggplant slices with two-thirds of the olive oil, then grill, turning once, until charred in places, about 5 minutes. (You will need to do this in two batches.)
3 Meanwhile, heat the remaining oil in a large, nonstick frying pan over medium heat. Add the tomatoes and chili and season with salt and pepper. Fry until softened, 2 to 3 minutes.
4 Make a layer of half the eggplant slices in a baking dish and spoon half of the tomato mixture on top. Scatter the mozzarella over the tomato mixture, then make a second layer of eggplant.
5 Scatter the remaining tomato mixture, the walnuts and parsley over the top. Bake until heated through and the mozzarella starts to melt, 5 to 8 minutes. Serve with slices of ciabatta bread and a watercress salad.

INDEX

apples:
  Warm caramelized apple & goat cheese
    salad 78
artichokes:
  Artichoke, pine nut & Parmesan tart 156
  Bresaola & artichoke salad 16
  Polenta with artichoke sauce 104
asparagus:
  Scrambled eggs with asparagus 48
avocado:
  Bean chile with avocado cream 105
  Crisp fish with avocado salsa 69
  Hot chicken sticks with guacamole 60
  Picadillo with avocado salsa 115
  Smoked chicken, avocado & walnut salad 12
  Smoked trout, sugar snap & avocado salad 20

bacon:
  Chickpea, bacon & spinach stew 37
  Spaghetti carbonara 37
beans:
  Bean chile with avocado cream 105
  Best beans on toast 33
  Cannellini bean & sausage stew 140
  Cheat's garlic shrimp & beans 22
  Chickpea, bacon & spinach stew 37
  Crisp bean cakes with chili-lime dip 150
  Lima bean & chorizo pan-fry 64
  Pepper-crusted tuna with bean compôte 123
  Potato, chard & green bean braise 155
  Spicy coconut & chickpea soup 82
  Tuna & bean salad 19
  Zucchini & cannellini bean soup 130
beef:
  Bresaola & artichoke salad 16
  Caribbean blackened beef with mango
    mayonnaise 40
  Ginger beef & cashew noodles 94
  Minute steaks with blue cheese sauce 16
  Picadillo with avocado salsa 115
  Seared steaks with romesco-style sauce 94
  Sloppy joes 93
  Spiced beef & bean threads salad 116
  Spicy beef in lettuce cups 38
  Steak in Marsala 142
  Steak with Marsala mustard cream 68
Belgian endive:
  Blue cheese, endive & walnut salad 29
blackberries:
  Lamb steaks with blackberry sauce 67
broccoli:
  Savory corn tartlets 128
broccoli raab:
  Broccoli raab orecchiette 106
bruschetta:
  Broiled sardines on bruschetta 42
  Garlic mushrooms on rosemary
    bruschetta 30
  Ricotta & tomato bruschetta 30

butter:
  Lemony butter sauce 122

cabbage:
  Twice-cooked crisp chicken with sesame
    cabbage 87
capers:
  Caper & lemon-butter linguine 32
  Caper mayonnaise 99
  Tuna carpaccio with caper dressing 19
  Tuna cakes with tomato-caper sauce 149
cashew nuts:
  Ginger beef & cashew noodles 94
chard:
  Potato, chard & green bean braise 155
cheese:
  Artichoke, pine nut & Parmesan tart 156
  Arugula & Parmesan penne 56
  Baked chicken breasts in tomato &
    mascarpone 135
  Blue cheese, endive & walnut salad 29
  Box-baked Camembert 79
  Cheese & prosciutto crostata 90
  Cheesy chicken wrapped in pancetta 111
  Cheesy sweet potatoes 129
  Chèvre toasts with cranberry relish 28
  Eggplant, mozzarella & tomato bake 156
  Feta & corn fritters with salsa 126
  Fig, lentil & feta salad 126
  Fig & mozzarella salad with warm vincotto
    dressing 26
  Grilled halloumi, pistachio & watermelon
    salad 52
  Hot mortadella panini 14
  Minted couscous & feta salad 50
  Minute steaks with blue cheese sauce 16
  Mozzarella, tomato & arugula salad 26
  Open ricotta lasagne 57
  Pan-fried halloumi with quick tomato
    sauce 28
  Pan-grilled smoked salmon wraps 43
  Pancetta-wrapped cheese with spinach
    salad 63
  Parmesan, sage & peppercorn pasta 54
  Parmesan-crusted cod with buttered
    corn 122
  Pasta carbonara 37
  Pea, rosemary & mascarpone risotto 152
  Peach & feta salad with lime dressing 53
  Piadina pizza margarita 57
  "Poor man's Parmesan" pasta 80
  Pork burgers with blue cheese and red
    onion salsa 139
  Prosciutto, pecorino & leaf salad 14
  Ricotta & fresh herb frittata 130
  Ricotta & tomato bruschetta 30
  Roquefort, arugula & pita salad 53
  Swiss cheese fondue 104
  Three-cheese phyllo tarts 79

Tomato, ricotta & spinach strudel 151
Warm caramelized apple & goat cheese
  salad 78
chicken:
  Baked chicken breasts in tomato &
    mascarpone 135
  Balinese spicy chicken soup 88
  Cheesy chicken wrapped in pancetta 111
  Chicken & basil stir-fry 36
  Chicken & coconut soup 60
  Chicken cutlets in rich tomato sauce 87
  Chicken noodle soup 13
  Golden chicken goujons with mayo 110
  Grilled gremolata-crusted chicken 86
  Hot chicken sticks with guacamole 60
  Prosciutto-wrapped chicken breasts 134
  Sesame chicken salad 62
  Smoked chicken, avocado & walnut salad 12
  Sticky chicken with almond couscous 134
  Thai chicken curry 110
  Twice-cooked crisp chicken with sesame
    cabbage 87
chickpeas:
  Chickpea, bacon & spinach stew 37
  Spicy coconut & chickpea soup 82
chilies:
  Bean chile with avocado cream 105
  Chili & garlic vinaigrette 120
  Chili-fried eggs with tomato toasts 50
  Chili hoisin noodles with tofu 56
  Crisp bean cakes with chili-lime dip 150
  Fish in chili broth 72
  Herb sausage cakes with chili greens 114
  Quick chili noodles 33
  Roasted red mullet with chili & garlic
    vinaigrette 120
  Spaghettini with chili oil & garlic 54
  Tomato & chili mussels 100
chorizo:
  Lima bean & chorizo pan-fry 64
  Migas con chorizo 64
cilantro:
  Cilantro & garlic dip 91
  Lime & cilantro dressing 46
clams:
  Linguine with clams & white wine 125
coconut:
  Chicken & coconut soup 60
  Coconut turkey stir-fry 36
  Fish koftas with coconut rice 124
  Pan-grilled salmon with coconut spinach 71
  Spicy coconut & chickpea soup 82
  Vegetable curry with coconut rice 154
cod:
  Parmesan-crusted cod with buttered
    corn 122
corn:
  Crab & corn cakes with mango salsa 146
  Feta & corn fritters with salsa 126

Parmesan-crusted cod with buttered
    corn 122
Savory corn tartlets 128
couscous:
    Lamb kebabs with jewelled couscous 141
    Minted couscous & feta salad 50
    Moroccan-spiced fish with couscous 120
    Sticky chicken with almond couscous 134
crab:
    Crab & angel hair pasta 22
    Crab & corn cakes with mango salsa 146
cucumber:
    Blackened fish with tzatziki 119
    Ginger beef & cashew noodles 94
    Seared salmon with cucumber relish 42

duck:
    Crisp duck lasagne 136
    Golden ginger duck 62
    Honeyed duck in pomegranate sauce 136

eggplant:
    Eggplant, mozzarella & tomato bake 156
eggs:
    Baked eggs in smoked salmon cups 72
    Cherry tomato clafoutis 131
    Chili-fried eggs with tomato toasts 50
    Eggs florentine 48
    Feta & corn fritters with salsa 126
    Ham with lentils & poached eggs 140
    Ricotta & fresh herb frittata 130
    Salade niçoise 96
    Scrambled eggs with asparagus 48
    Spinach, prosciutto & egg salad 13
    Two-pepper pipérade 103

fennel:
    Seared salmon, fennel & sugar snap
        salad 71
figs:
    Fig & mozzarella salad with warm vincotto
        dressing 26
    Fig, lentil & feta salad 126
fish:
    Blackened fish with tzatziki 119
    Crisp fish goujons 99
    Crisp fish with avocado salsa 69
    Fish in chili broth 72
    Fish koftas with coconut rice 124
    Fish tagine 149
    Lemon & olive roasted fish 119
    Moroccan-spiced fish with couscous 120
    see also cod; salmon, etc

garlic:
    Chili & garlic vinaigrette 120
    Cilantro & garlic dip 91
    Garlic & ginger pork 38
    Garlic mushrooms on rosemary
        bruschetta 30
    Garlic sauce 93
    Spaghettini with chili oil & garlic 54
ginger:
    Garlic & ginger pork 38

Ginger beef & cashew noodles 94
Golden ginger duck 62

haddock:
    Smoked haddock gratin 145
ham:
    Crisp ham salad with honey & mustard
        dressing 89
    Grilled ham steaks with pineapple & mint
        relish 113
    Ham with lentils & poached eggs 140
    see also prosciutto

lamb:
    Glazed lamb chops with garlic sauce 93
    Lamb kebabs with jewelled couscous
        141
    Lamb steaks with blackberry sauce 67
    Seared lamb with cinnamon onions 141
    Souvlaki with cilantro & garlic yogurt
        dip 91
    Sticky lamb satay 114
    Thai-sizzled lamb 92
lemongrass:
    Lime & lemongrass pork 63
lemons:
    Lemon & basil veal cutlets 40
    Lemon & olive roasted fish 119
    Lobster & herb salad with lemon mayo 98
    Roasted meatballs in lemon & bay 142
    Salmon in lemony butter sauce 122
    Spiced lemon scallops 47
    Warm citrus dressing 68
lentils:
    Fig, lentil & feta salad 126
    Ham with lentils & poached eggs 140
    Spicy red lentils 155
    Trout fillets & lentils in warm citrus
        dressing 68
limes:
    Chili-lime dip 150
    Lime & cilantro dressing 46
    Lime & lemongrass pork 63
    Lime dressing 53
    Salt & chili squid with lime 21
lobster:
    Lobster & herb salad with lemon
        mayo 98

mango:
    Caribbean blackened beef with mango
        mayonnaise 40
    Mango salsa 146
mayonnaise:
    Caper mayonnaise 99
    Herb & garlic mayonnaise 110
    Lemon mayonnaise 98
mint:
    Fresh mint & pea pesto cavatappi 80
    Minted couscous & feta salad 50
    Pineapple & mint relish 113
miso:
    Miso & tofu soup with wontons 83
    Spiced salmon in noodle miso broth 75

mushrooms:
    Creamed mushrooms with polenta 150
    Garlic mushrooms on rosemary
        bruschetta 30
    Pork in mushroom & mustard sauce 139
mussels:
    Tomato & chilli mussels 100
mustard:
    Honey & mustard dressing 89
    Pork in mushroom & mustard sauce 139
    Steak with Marsala mustard cream 68

noodles:
    Chicken noodle soup 13
    Chili hoisin noodles with tofu 56
    Ginger beef & cashew noodles 94
    Quick chili noodles 33
    Spiced beef & bean threads salad 116
    Spiced salmon in noodle miso broth 75

olives:
    Lemon & olive roasted fish 119
    Salade niçoise 96
    Seared tuna with tomato & olive sauce 69
onions:
    Red onion salsa 139
    Seared lamb with cinnamon onions 141
oranges:
    Cranberry relish 28
    Trout fillets in warm citrus dressing 68

pancetta:
    Cheesy chicken wrapped in pancetta 111
    Pancetta-wrapped cheese & spinach
        salad 63
    Pasta carbonara 37
papaya:
    Salsa 126
parsnips:
    Curried parsnip soup 154
pasta:
    Arugula & Parmesan penne 56
    Big-bowl minestrone 82
    Broccoli raab orecchiette 106
    Caper & lemon-butter linguine 32
    Crab & angel hair pasta 22
    Fresh mint & pea pesto cavatappi 80
    Linguine with clams & white wine 125
    Open ricotta lasagne 57
    Parmesan, sage & peppercorn pasta 54
    "Poor man's Parmesan" pasta 80
    Sausage & red wine fusilli 88
    Smoked salmon tagliatelle 20
    Spaghetti carbonara 37
    Spaghettini with chili oil & garlic 54
    Walnut pesto linguine 106
    Zucchini & raisin penne 129
pea shoots:
    Seared scallop & pea shoot salad 21
peach:
    Peach & feta salad with lime dressing 53
peas:
    Fresh mint & pea pesto cavatappi 80
    Pea, rosemary & mascarpone risotto 152

Seared salmon, fennel & sugar snap salad 71
Shrimp & three-pea stir-fry 25
Smoked trout, sugar snap & avocado
    salad 20
peppers:
    Salade niçoise 96
    Two-pepper pipérade 103
pesto:
    Fresh mint & pea pesto cavatappi 80
    Walnut pesto linguine 106
piadine:
    Open sardine piadina 75
    Piadina pizza margarita 57
pine nuts:
    Artichoke, pine nut & Parmesan tart 156
pineapple:
    Pineapple & mint relish 113
    Sweet soy & pineapple pork 91
    Thai shrimp & pineapple curry 76
pistachio nuts:
    Grilled halloumi, pistachio & watermelon
        salad 52
pizzas:
    Broiled salami pita pizzas 15
    Piadina pizza margarita 57
polenta:
    Creamed mushrooms with polenta 150
    Crisp fish goujons 99
    Polenta with artichoke sauce 104
pork:
    Garlic & ginger pork 38
    Herby pork skewers 67
    Lime & lemongrass pork 63
    Pork burgers with blue cheese and red
        onion salsa 139
    Pork in mushroom & mustard sauce 139
    Pork tonnato 112
    Pork with prunes 112
    Sweet soy & pineapple pork 91
potatoes:
    Potato, chard & green bean braise 155
    Roasted sea bass with stoved potatoes
        146
prosciutto:
    Cheese & prosciutto crostata 90
    Prosciutto, pecorino & green leaf salad 14
    Prosciutto-wrapped chicken parcels 134
    Spinach, prosciutto & egg salad 13
prunes:
    Pork with prunes 112

quinoa:
    Lemon & parsley quinoa 119

raisins:
    Zucchini & raisin penne 129
red mullet:
    Roasted red mullet with chili & garlic
        vinaigrette 120
rice:
    Fish koftas with coconut rice 124
    Pea, rosemary & mascarpone risotto 152
    Squash-blossom risotto 152
    Vegetable curry with coconut rice 154

salami:
    Broiled salami pita pizzas 15
salmon:
    Baked eggs in smoked salmon cups 72
    Mini salmon en croûtes 145
    Pan-grilled salmon with coconut spinach 71
    Pan-grilled smoked salmon wraps 43
    Salmon in lemony butter sauce 122
    Seared salmon with cucumber relish 42
    Seared salmon, fennel & sugar snap salad 71
    Sesame-crusted salmon with dip 96
    Smoked salmon tagliatelle 20
    Spiced salmon in noodle miso broth 75
sardines:
    Broiled sardines on bruschetta 42
    Open sardine piadina 75
sausages/sausage:
    Cannellini bean & sausage stew 140
    Herb sausage patties with chili greens 114
    Lima bean & chorizo pan-fry 64
    Migas con chorizo 64
    Sausage & red wine fusilli 88
scallops:
    Seared scallop & pea shoot salad 21
    Spiced lemon scallops 47
sea bass:
    Baked sea bass in newspaper 124
    Roasted sea bass with stoved potatoes 146
    Sea bass with creamy dill sauce 99
sesame seeds:
    Sesame chicken salad 62
    Sesame-crusted salmon with dip 96
    Twice-cooked crisp chicken with sesame
        cabbage 87
shellfish:
    Mixed shellfish Colombo 100
shrimp:
    Cheat's garlic shrimp & beans 22
    Creole shrimp 77
    Fish koftas 124
    Moroccan-spiced shrimp 76
    Shrimp & three-pea stir-fry 25
    Shrimp laksa 44
    Spiced tomato shrimp 25
    Thai shrimp & pineapple curry 76
spinach:
    Chickpea, bacon & spinach stew 37
    Eggs florentine 48
    Pan-grilled salmon with coconut spinach 71
    Pancetta-wrapped cheese with spinach
        salad 63
    Spinach, prosciutto & egg salad 13
    Tomato, ricotta & spinach strudel 151
squid:
    Crisp-crumbed squid with aioli 47
    Salt & chili squid with lime 21
    Sizzled squid with lime & cilantro
        dressing 46
sweet potatoes:
    Cheesy sweet potatoes 129

tofu:
    Chili hoisin noodles with tofu 56
    Miso & tofu soup with wontons 83

tomatoes:
    Baked chicken breasts in tomato &
        mascarpone 135
    Cherry tomato clafoutis 131
    Chicken cutlets in rich tomato sauce 87
    Chickpea, bacon & spinach stew 37
    Chili-fried eggs with tomato toasts 50
    Eggplant, mozzarella & tomato bake 156
    Mozzarella, tomato & arugula salad 26
    Open ricotta lasagne 57
    Pan-fried halloumi with quick tomato
        sauce 28
    Pan-grilled smoked salmon wraps 43
    Ricotta & tomato bruschetta 30
    Seared tuna with tomato & olive sauce 69
    Sloppy joes 93
    Spiced tomato shrimp 25
    Tomato & chili mussels 100
    Tomato, ricotta & spinach strudel 151
    Tomato tarte tatin 151
    Tuna & cherry tomato spiedini 44
    Tuna cakes with tomato-caper sauce 149
trout:
    Smoked trout, sugar snap & avocado
        salad 20
    Trout & lentils in warm citrus dressing 68
tuna:
    Pepper-crusted tuna with bean compôte 123
    Pork tonnato 112
    Salade niçoise 96
    Seared tuna with tomato & olive sauce 69
    Tuna & bean salad 19
    Tuna & cherry tomato spiedini 44
    Tuna cakes with tomato-caper sauce 149
    Tuna carpaccio with caper dressing 19
turkey:
    Coconut turkey stir-fry 36
    Golden turkey cutlets with tarator 135

veal:
    Lemon & basil veal cutlets 40
    Roasted meatballs in lemon & bay 142
    Veal chops in sage & red wine 116
vegetables:
    Big bowl minestrone 82
    Vegetable curry with coconut rice 154
    see also peas; zucchini, etc

walnuts:
    Blue cheese, endive & walnut salad 29
    Smoked chicken, avocado & walnut salad 12
    Walnut pesto linguine 106
watermelon:
    Grilled halloumi, pistachio & watermelon
        salad 52

yogurt:
    Blackened fish with tzatziki 119
    Souvlaki with cilantro & garlic yogurt dip 91

zucchini:
    Squash-blossom risotto 152
    Zucchini & cannellini bean soup 130
    Zucchini & raisin penne 129